NATIVE AMERICAN

TALES

RETOLD BY:

DEBRA KUHL

Also Written By Debra Kuhl

Black Bert the Pirate

Sammy's Magic Carpet Ride

Camp Utopia

I Double Dog Date You

For my Grandson, Gavin Klar.

ACKNOWLEDGMENT

The American Indian has always been a lover of nature and a close observer of her many moods. The habits of the birds and animals, the voices of the winds and waters, the flickering of the shadows, and the mystic radiance of the moonlight, all appealed to them. Gradually, the American Indian formulated within himself fanciful reasons for the myriad manifestations of the Mighty Mother and her many children; and a poet by instinct, he framed odd stories with which to convey his explanations to others. These stories have been handed down from father to son, with little variation, through countless generations, until the white man slaughtered the buffalo, took to himself the open country, and left the American Indian little better than a beggar. But the tribal storyteller has passed, and only here and there is to be found a patriarch who loves the legends of other days.

I would like to express my deepest appreciation to the many Native Americans tribes who have kept these stories alive making this book possible. During my research, I listened to many American Indian story tellers retelling these legends. These stories have been recorded exactly as the story teller told them. Neither grammar nor sentence structure have been changed in an effort to keep the original tales.

TABLE OF CONTENTS

THE SUN DANCE WHEEL

(Arapaho)

At one time the whole world was covered with water. It was everywhere, no matter where one looked.

The water did not stop a man carrying Flat Pipe, his companion and counselor, from walking across the waters for four days and nights. The man wanted to treat his pipe in the best way, so he gave much thought to this subject. He thought for six days and finally decided that in order to provide a good home for Flat Pipe there should be land and the good company of creatures.

So, on the seventh day the man set out to find land among all the water, calling to the four directions as he went. From the four directions came many animal helpers, and with their help man found a land home. He put the Four Old Men in each of the four directions to control the winds. Now, the land would also provide a place for a Sun Dance of ceremony and thanksgiving every year.

A garter snake came to the man, and the man said, "Oh, you will be a great comfort to the people and have a great place in the Sun Dance as the Sacred Wheel to represent the waters that surround this earth."

He then looked again to all around him for help and many offered.

Long Stick, a bush with flexible limbs and dark bark, came and said "I offer myself for the wheel for the good of all."

All approved so Long Stick was made into the ring of the Sacred Wheel, representing the circle that is the Sun.

The eagle soared by and said, "My strength is great enough to carry me above the earth and water as I fly on the winds of the four directions. Please take my feathers to represent the Four Old Men."

The man was pleased, and told all that four bunches of eagle feathers would forever be tied to the wheel to honor the desire of the eagle and anyone who would ever offer an eagle feather as a gift.

Once the man shaped the Sacred Wheel, he painted it in the image of garter snake and placed the feathers in the position of the Four Old Men, Northwest, Northeast, Southeast and Southwest, who rule the directions and control the winds and to represent the Thunderbird who brings the rain. To further enhance the wheel, the man added groups of stars, painting special images of the Sun, the Moon and the Milky Way. Blue beads tied on represented the sky.

When finished, the man thanked the garter snake for serving his people in this way with the creation of the wheel that symbolizes all creation.

HOW MEDICINE MAN RESURRECTED BUFFALO

(Arapaho)

At one time an Arapaho Medicine Man named Black Robe wanted very much to be able to make magic because his people were very hungry. How could he lure the Buffaloes back to the Arapaho hunting grounds? Buffalo meat was their main food.

Black Robe decided to ask Cedar Tree for his help. "Go west and hunt Buffalo for our people. Try very hard to find at least one Buffalo."

Cedar Tree hunted hard as he was asked to do. After a long time, he saw some black objects at a distance. "Could they be Buffalos?" he wondered.

Encouraged, he walked faster, but as he drew closer, he was less sure the black objects were Buffalos. Suddenly, he saw the black objects fly toward the sky. By then, Cedar Tree seemed certain the objects were oversized ravens.

Disappointed, he returned to his village, reporting to Black Robe what he had seen. The Medicine Man scolded him for not believing that what he had seen were Buffalos.

"If you had only believed strong enough, the Buffalos would not have changed to Ravens," said Black Robe.

By now the Arapahos were desperately hungry. One woman on the verge of starving made soup from the soles of her moccasins. The next day her uncle, Trying Bear, set out early to hunt for anything edible. He had no weapons. Fortunately, on the way he met Black Robe who loaned him a bow and some arrows.

"Tomorrow morning, I will come to your tent to learn of your success," said Black Robe. "You must even try to find a dried Buffalo, if not a live one."

After hunting a long time to the Northwest, Trying Bear finally found a dried Buffalo. He ran home swiftly to tell his people. Black Robe painted his white pony black and wrapped a black buffalo robe about himself. He stuck his lucky Eagle feather in his hair, mounted his black pony, and took off in a rush to find the dried Buffalo.

"Follow me, Trying Bear," Black Robe called.

Because he wanted to see what Black Robe would do with the dried Buffalo, Trying Bear followed rapidly. Medicine Man arrived sometime during the middle of the day at the place of the dead Buffalo. He dismounted, took aim with his magic Eagle feather, and threw it straight at the body. Immediately, a live Buffalo jumped to its feet!

Black Robe turned and looked at Trying Bear.

"Shoot it!" commanded Medicine Man.

Trying Bear shot it dead.

"Let's skin it and carry everything eatable back to our people," said Black Robe.

A feast of thanksgiving and celebration followed. Black Robe had saved his people from starvation.

THE LAME WARRIOR AND THE SKELETON

(Arapaho)

In the days before horses, a party of young Arapahos set off on foot one fall morning in search of game in the western mountains. They carried heavy packs of food and spare moccasins, and one day as they were crossing the rocky bed of a shallow stream a young warrior felt a sudden sharp pain in his ankle. The ankle swelled and the pain grew worse until they pitched camp that night.

The next morning the warrior's ankle was swollen so badly that it was impossible for him to continue the journey with the others. His companions decided it was best to leave him. They cut young willows and tall grass to make a thatched shelter for him, and after the shelter was finished, they collected a pile of dry wood so that he could keep a fire burning.

"When your ankle gets well," they told him, "don't try to follow us. Go back to our village, and await our return."

After several lonely days, the lame warrior tested his ankle, but it was still too painful to walk upon. And then one night a heavy snowstorm fell, virtually imprisoning him in the shelter. Because he had been unable to kill any game, his food supply was almost gone.

A few days later he looked out and saw a large herd of buffalo rooting in the snow for grass quite close to his shelter. Reaching for his bow and arrow, he shot the fattest one and killed it. He then crawled out of the shelter to the buffalo, skinned it, and brought in the meat. After preparing a bed of coals, he placed a section of ribs in the fire for roasting.

Night had fallen by the time the ribs were cooked, and just as the lame warrior was reaching for a piece to eat, he heard footsteps crunching on the frozen snow. The steps came nearer and nearer to the closed flap of the shelter.

"Who can that be?" he said to himself. "I am here alone and unable to run, but I shall defend myself if need be." He reached for his bow and arrow.

A moment later the flap opened and a Skeleton clothed in a tanned buffalo robe stood there looking down at the lame warrior.

The buffalo robe was pinned tight at the neck so that only the skull was visible above and skeleton feet below. Frightened by this Skelton, the warrior turned his eyes away from it.

"You must not be frightened of me," the Skeleton said in a hoarse voice. "I have taken pity on you. Now you must take pity on me. Give me a piece of those roast ribs to eat, for I am very hungry."

Still very much alarmed by the presence of the Skeleton, the lame warrior offered a large piece of meat to an extended bony hand. He was astonished to see the Skeleton chew the food with its bared teeth and swallow it.

"It was I who gave you the pain in your ankle," said the Skeleton. "It was I who caused your ankle to swell so that you could not continue on the hunt. If you had gone on with your friends you would have been killed. The day they left you here, an enemy war party made a charge upon them, and they were all killed. I am the one who saved your life."

Again, the Skeleton's bony hand reached out, this time to rub the warrior's ankle. The pain and swelling vanished at once. "Now you can walk again," the Skeleton said. "Your enemies are all around, but if you will follow me, I can lead you safely back to your village."

At dawn they left the shelter and started off across the snow, the Skeleton leading the way. They walked through deep woods, along icy streams, and over high hills. Late in the afternoon the Skeleton led the warrior up a steep ridge. When the warrior reached the top, the Skeleton had vanished, but down in the valley below he could see the smokes of teepees in his Arapaho village.

THE ORIGIN OF CORN AND GAME

(Cherokee)

A man and a woman reared a large family of children with very little trouble providing food for them. Every morning the father went forth and very soon returned bringing with him a deer, a turkey, or some other animal or fowl. At the same time the mother went out and soon returned with a large basket filled with ears of corn which she shelled and pounded in a mortar, thus making meal for bread.

When the children grew up, seeing what obvious food was provided for them, they talked to each other about it, wondering that they never saw such things as their parents brought in. At last one suggested to watch when their parents went out and to follow them.

Accordingly, the next morning their plan was carried out. The sons followed the father saw him stop a short distance from the cabin and turn over a large stone that appeared to be carelessly leaned against another. On looking closely, the sons saw an entrance to a large cave, and in it were many different kinds of animals and birds, such as their father had sometimes brought in for food. The father standing at the opening of the cave called a Deer, which was lying at some distance back of some other animals. It rose immediately as it heard the call and came close to their father. He picked it up, closed the mouth of the cave, and returned, not once seeming to suspect what his sons had saw.

When the father was fairly out of sight, his sons, rejoicing how they had outwitted him, left their hiding place and went to the cave, saying they would show their parents that they, too, could bring in something. They moved the stone away, though it was very heavy and they were required to use all their united strength. When the cave was opened, the animals, instead of waiting to be picked up, all made a rush for the entrance, and leaping past the frightened and confused boys, scattered in all directions and disappeared in the wilderness, while the guilty sons could do nothing but gaze in stunned amazement as they saw them escape. There were animals of all kinds, large and small, Buffalo, Deer, Elk, Antelope, Raccoons, and Squirrels; even Catamounts and Panthers, Wolves and Foxes, and many others, all fleeing together. At the same time Birds of every kind were seen flying from the opening, all in the same wild confusion as the quadrupeds, Turkeys, Geese, Swans, Ducks, Quails, Eagles, Hawks, and Owls.

The daughters who followed the mother saw her enter a small cabin, which they had never seen before, and close the door. The daughters found a small crack through which they could peer. They saw the woman place a basket on the ground and standing over it shake herself enthusiastically, jumping up and down, when lo and behold large ears of corn began to fall in the basket. When it was filled, she took it up and, placing it on her head, came out, fastened the door, and prepared their breakfast as usual. When the meal had been finished in silence the father spoke to his sons, telling them that he was aware of what they had done; that now he must die and they would be have to provide for themselves. He made bows and arrows for them, and then sent them to hunt for the animals which they had turned loose.

Then the mother told the daughters that as they had found out her secret, she could do nothing more for them; that she would die, and they must drag her body around over the ground; that wherever her body was dragged corn would come up. Of this they were to make their bread. She told the children that they must always save some corn for seed and plant every year.

THE FIRST STRAWBERRIES

(Cherokee)

In the beginning of the world, the Heaven created First Man and First Woman. Together they built a lodge at the edge of a dense forest. They were very happy together; but like all people do at times, they began to argue.

Finally, First Woman became so angry she said she was leaving and never coming back. At that moment, First Man really didn't care. First Woman started walking westward down the path through the forest. She never looked back.

As the day grew later, First Man began to worry. At last, he started down the same path in search of his wife. The Sun looked down on First Man and took pity on him. The Sun asked First Man if he was still angry with First Woman. First Man said he was not angry any more. The Sun asked if he would like to have First Woman back First Man readily agreed he did.

The Sun found First Woman still walking down the path toward the West. So, to persuade her to stop, the Sun caused to grow beneath her feet lovely blueberries. The blueberries were large and ripe. First Woman paid no attention but kept walking down the path toward the West.

Further down the path the Sun caused to grow some luscious blackberries. The berries were very black and plump. First Woman looked neither left nor right but kept walking down the path toward the west.

At last the Sun caused to grow a plant that had never grown on the earth before. The plant covered the ground in front of First Woman. Suddenly she became aware of a fragrance she had never known. Stopping she looked down at her feet. Growing beside her feet was a plant with shiny green leaves, lovely white flowers with the largest most luscious red berries she had ever seen. First

Woman stopped to pick one. Hmmm…she had never tasted anything quite like this! It was so sweet.

As First Woman ate the berry, the anger she felt began to fade away. She thought again of her husband and how they had parted in anger. She missed him and wanted to go back home.

First Woman began to gather some of the berries. When she had all she could carry, she turned toward the East and started back down the path. Soon she met First Man. Together they shared the berries, and then hand in hand, they walked back to their lodge.

Strawberries are often kept in Cherokee homes to remind us not to argue and are a symbol of good luck.

ORIGIN OF DISEASE AND MEDICINE

(Cherokee)

In the old days the Beasts, Birds, Fishes, Insects and plants could all talk. They and the Indians lived together in peace and friendship. But as time went on the Indians increased so fast that their settlement spread over the whole earth, and the poor animals found themselves cramped for room. This was bad enough, but to make it worse, Indians invented bows, knives, spears, and hooks, and began to kill the larger animals, Birds, and Fishes for their flesh or their skins, while the smaller creatures, such as the Frogs and Worms, were crushed and trampled upon without thought, out of pure carelessness or dislike. So, the animals resolved to consult upon measures for their common safety.

The Bears were the first to meet in council in their cave under the mountain, and the old White Bear Chief presided. After each in turn had complained of the way in which the Indian killed their friends, ate their flesh, and used their skins for his own purposes, it was decided to begin war at once against him. Someone asked what weapons the Indian used to destroy them.

"Bows and arrow" cried all the Bears.

"What are they made of?" was the next question.

"The bow of wood, and the string of our entrails," replied one of the Bears.

It was then proposed they make a bow and some arrows and see if they could not use the same weapons against the Indian himself. So, one Bear got a piece of locust wood and another sacrificed himself for the good of the rest in order to furnish his entrails for the string. But when everything was ready and the first Bear stepped up to make the trial, it was found that in letting the arrow fly after drawing back the bow, his long claws caught in the string and spoiled the shot. This was frustrating, but someone suggested that they might trim his claws, which was done, and on a second trial it was found that the arrow went straight to the mark. Here the old White Bear Chief, protested, saying it was necessary that they should have long claws in order to be able to climb trees.

"One of us has already died to furnish the bow string and if we now cut off our claws, we must all starve together. It is better to trust to the teeth and claws that nature gave us, for it is plain that the Indian's weapons were not intended for us," said old White Bear Chief.

No one could think of any better plan, so the old White Bear Chief dismissed the council and the Bears went to the woods and thickets without having concerted any way to prevent the increase of the Indian race. Had the decision of the council been different, Indians should now be at war with the Bears, but as it is, the Indian does not even ask the Bear's permission when he kills one.

The Deer next held a council under their Chief, the Little Deer, and after some talk, devised to send rheumatism to every Indian who should kill one of them unless he took care to ask their pardon for the wrongdoing. They sent notice of their decision to the nearest settlement of Indians and told them at the same time what to do when necessity forced them to kill one of the Deer tribe. Now, whenever the Indian shoots a Deer, their Chief, the Little Deer, who is swift as the wind and ca not be injured, runs quickly up to the spot and, bending over the bloodstains, asks the spirit of the Deer if it has heard the prayer of the Indian for pardon. if the reply be Yes, all is well, and their Chief, the Little Deer goes on his way; but if the reply be No, he follows on the trail of the Indian, guided by the drops of blood on the ground, until he arrives at his lodge, when their Chief, the Little Deer enters invisibly and strikes the Indian with rheumatism, so that he becomes at once a helpless cripple. no Indian who has regard for his health ever forgets to ask pardon of the Deer for killing it, although some Indians who have not learned the prayer may try to turn aside their Chief, the Little Deer from his search by building a fire behind them in the trail.

Next came, the Fishes and Reptile, who had their own complaints against the Indian. They held council together and determined to make their victims dream of snakes twining about them in slimy folds and blowing foul breath in their faces, or to make them dream of eating raw or decaying fish, so that they would lose appetite, sicken and die. This is why people dream about snakes and fish.

Finally, the Birds, Insects, and smaller animals came together for the same purpose, and the Grub Worm was Chief of the council. It was decided that each in turn should give a vote, and then they would vote on the question as to whether or not the Indian was guilty. Seven votes should be enough to condemn him. After they condemn the Indian's cruelty and injustice toward the other animals and they would then vote in favor of death.

The Frog spoke first, saying, "We must do something to check the increase of the race, or the Indian will become so numerous that we will be crowded from off the earth. See how they have kicked me about because I'm ugly, as they say, until my back is covered with sores;" and here he showed the spots on his skin.

Next came the Bird, no one remembers which one it was who condemned The Indian. "Because he burns my feet off," meaning the way in which Indians barbecue birds by impaling them on a stick set over the fire, so that their feathers and tender feet are singed off.

Others followed with their injuries. The Ground Squirrel was the only one that did say a good word for the Indian, who seldom hurt him because he was so small, but this made the others so angry that they fell upon the Ground Squirrel and tore him with their claws, and the stripes are on this back to this day.

The animals began then to devise and name so many new diseases, one after another, even ones that had not yet been created at last failed them.

The Grub Worm grew continuously more pleased as the name of each disease was called off, until at last they reached the end of the list, when someone suggested making menstruation sometimes fatal to women. On this he rose up in his place and cried "Thanks! I'm glad some more of them will die, for they are getting so thick that the tread on me." The thought fairly made him shake with joy, so that he fell over backward and could not get on his feet again, but had to wriggle off on his back, as the Grub Worm has done ever since.

When the Plants, who were friendly to the Indian, heard what had been done by the animals, they determined to defeat their' evil plan. Each Tree, Shrub, and Herb, even down to the Grasses, and Mosses, said, "I shall help the Indian when he calls upon me in his need.

From this came medicine; and the plants, every one of which has its use if only the Indians knew it. They furnish the remedy to counteract the evil created by the revengeful animals. Even weeds were made for some good purpose, which the Indians must find out for themselves. When the Medicine Man does not know what medicine to use for a sick man, the spirit of the plants tells him.

HOW THEY BROUGHT BACK THE TOBACCO

(Cherokee)

In the beginning of the world, when Indians and animals were all the same, there was only one tobacco plant, to which they all came for their tobacco until the Geese stole it and carried it far away to the South. The Indians were suffering without it, and there was one old woman who grew so thin and weak that everybody said she would soon die unless she could get tobacco to keep her alive.

Different animals offered to go for it, one after another, the larger ones first and then the smaller ones, but the Geese killed every one before he could get to the plant. After the others, the little Mole tried to reach it by going under the ground, but the Geese saw his track and killed him as he came out.

At last the Hummingbird offered, but the others said he was entirely too small and might as well stay at home. He begged them to let him try, so they showed him a plant in a field and told him to let them see how he would go about it. The next moment he was gone and they saw him sitting on the plant, and then in a moment he was back again, but no one had seen him going or coming, because he was so swift.

"This is the way I'll do it, "said the Hummingbird, so they let him try.

He flew off to the East, and when he came in sight of the tobacco the Geese were watching it, but they could not see him because he was so small and flew so swiftly. He darted down on the plants and snatched off the top with the leaves and seeds, and was off again before the Geese knew what happened. Before he got home with the tobacco the old woman had fainted and they thought she was dead, but the Medicine Man blew the smoke into her nostrils, and with a cry of "Tobacco" she opened her eyes and was alive again.

WISE OWL

(Iroquois)

Once upon a time, a long time ago, the Everything Maker was very busy, making all the animals and all the plants and all the rocks and caverns and everything else that covered the earth.

When Owl was being made, he had been given a voice, two eyes, a head, a body and strong wings.

Owl was waiting his turn to be formed. "I want a long neck like Swan," Owl told the Everything Maker. "I want red feathers like the Cardinal and a beak like the Hawk."

"Yes, yes," mumbled the Everything Maker. "Whatever you want, but you must wait your turn." The Everything Maker looked sharply at Owl. "Your eyes are open again. You know that no one is allowed to watch me work. Turn around and close your eyes. I have no time for you now. I am busy forming Rabbit."

The Everything Maker turned his attention back to Rabbit who was shaking with nervousness. "What do you want, little rabbit?" the Everything Maker asked encouragingly.

"Long legs and ears," Rabbit spoke softly. "And fangs. Could I possibly have a fang or two, and claws? I would dearly love to have claws!"

The Everything Maker smiled. "I think we could manage some claws and fangs." He smoothed Rabbit's long legs and ears.

"Silly Rabbit!" the Owl hooted loudly. "Why don't you ask for something useful, like wisdom?"

"This is your last warning, Owl. Be quiet and wait your turn," yelled the Everything Maker.

Owl twisted around and glared at the Everything Maker. "You have to do it," he hooted. "You have to give us what we ask. I demand wisdom!"

"I warned you, Owl!" shouted the Everything Maker. He shoved Owl's head down into his body, which made Owl's neck disappear. He gave Owl a shake, which made Owl's eyes widen in fright. He pulled Owl's ears until they stuck out from his head.

The Everything Maker snapped his fingers. "I have made your ears big, the better to listen. I have made your eyes big, the better to see. I have made your neck short, the better to hold up your head. I have packed your head with wisdom, as you have asked. Now, use your wisdom and fly away before you lose what I have given."

Owl was no longer a fool. He flew quickly away, pouting and hooting.

The Everything Maker turned back to Rabbit, smiling gently. "Claws," he reminded himself. But Rabbit was gone. Rabbit had hopped hurriedly away, too afraid of the Everything Maker to stay for his fangs and claws.

As for Owl, he knew if he angered the Everything Maker again, he would lose all that he had gained. Even today, Owl only comes out at night, when the Everything Maker is fast asleep. As for Rabbit, his claws and fangs are waiting. Perhaps someday!

WHY RABBIT HAS A SHORT TAIL

(Cherokee)

Back when the world was young, Rabbit had a very long bushy tail. In fact, his tail was longer and bushier than the tail of Fox. Now Rabbit was very proud of his tail and he was constantly telling all the other animals about how beautiful his tail was. One day, Fox became so tired of hearing Rabbit brag about his tail that he decided to put an end to the boasting once and for all.

The weather was getting colder. One day it finally became so cold that the waters in the lake and streams froze. A few days later, Fox went down to the lake carrying four Fish. When he got to the lake, he cut a hole in the ice. He tied those four Fish to his tail, then sat down and waited for Rabbit to come.

Soon Rabbit came hopping over the top of the ridge. When Fox saw Rabbit, he quickly dropped his tail into the cold water.

Rabbit hopped right up to Fox and said, “What are you doing, Fox?”

Fox answered, “I’m fishing.”

Rabbit asked, “With your tail?”

Fox replied, “Oh yes, that’s the very best way to catch the most Fish.”

Rabbit said, “How long you been a fishing?”

Fox lied and said, “Oh, only about fifteen minutes.”

Rabbit asked, “Have you caught any Fish yet?”

Then Fox pulled up his tail, and there were those four Fish hanging on it.

Rabbit asked, “What do you plan to do with the Fish you catch?”

Fox said, “Well, I figure I’ll fish until I catch enough Fish to take to the Cherokee Village and then trade them in for a pair of beautiful tail combs. There is only one set of tail combs left and I really want them.” Fox could see that Rabbit was thinking.

Rabbit thought to himself, "If I fished all night long, I bet I would have enough Fish by morning to trade at the Cherokee Village. Then I could get those tail combs for myself."

Fox said, "It's getting late and I'm cold. I think I'll come back and fish some more in the morning. See ya, Rabbit" Then Fox loped off over the top of the ridge. As soon as Fox was out of sight, Rabbit dropped his tail down into the icy water of the lake.

Brrrrr, it was cold! But Rabbit thought, "Oh, No! I want those tail combs more than anything." So, he sat down on the hole in the ice and fished all night long.

Soon after the sun came up, Fox loped over the top of the ridge. He ran right up to Rabbit and said, "What are ya doing there, Rabbit?"

The teeth of Rabbit began to chatter. "I'm ffffissshing, Fffox." Fox asked, "Well have you caught any Fish?" Rabbit started to get up but he found he couldn't budge. He said, "Fffox you've ggott to helppp me. I'mmm ssstttuck."

So, Fox, with a big smile on his face walked behind Rabbit and gave Rabbit a big shove. Rabbit popped out of that hole and landed clear across the other side of the lake but his tail was still stuck in the frozen water. And that's why from that day until now; Rabbit has such a very short, short tail.

HOW THE RED BIRD GOT HIS COLOR

(Cherokee)

Raccoon loved to tease Wolf. One day Raccoon teased Wolf so much that Wolf became very angry. Wolf began to chase Raccoon through the woods. Raccoon, being the clever animal that he is, kept ahead of Wolf.

Raccoon came to a river. Instead of jumping in the river, he quickly climbed a tall tree and peered over a branch to see what Wolf would do next.

When Wolf came to the river, he saw the reflection of Raccoon in the water. Thinking that it was Raccoon, Wolf jumped in and tried to catch him. Wolf continued to search for Raccoon for such a long time that he became so tired he nearly drowned. Finally, tired and exhausted, Wolf climbed up the river bank and fell fast asleep. After a while, Raccoon quietly climbed down the tree and slipped over to the sleeping Wolf. While Wolf slept, Raccoon began to plaster the eyes of Wolf with mud. Then when he had finished, Raccoon ran off through the woods laughing to himself thinking of the clever trick he had played.

Later, Wolf woke up. He began to whine, "Oh, someone please help me. I can't see. I can't open my eyes." But no one came to help him.

At long last, Brown Bird heard the cries of Wolf. He flew over to Wolf and landed on his shoulder. He said, "What's the matter Brother Wolf? Can I help you?"

Wolf cried, "I can't open my eyes. Oh, please help me to see again."

Brown Bird said, "I'm just a little Brown Bird but I will help you if I can."

Wolf said, "Brown Bird, if you can help me to see again, I will take you to a magic rock that oozes red. We will paint your feathers red."

Brown Bird began pecking away at the dried mud on the eyes of Wolf. Soon Wolf could open his eyes again.

True to his promise Wolf said, “Thank you, my brother; now jump up onto my shoulder.” Away they ran through the woods to the rock that oozed red paint.

When they came to the rock, Wolf reached up and plucked a twig from a tree branch. He chewed the end of the twig until it was soft and pliable like the end of a paint brush. Then he dipped the end of the twig into the red paint and began to paint the feathers of Brown Bird.

When all of his feathers were red, Brown Bird flew off to show his family and friends how beautiful he was. That is why, from that day to this, you can see Red Bird flying around the woods in Cherokee country.

THE SACRED PIPE OF THE PEOPLE

(Cherokee)

Long ago, but not long after the world was new, a tribe of red skinned people came to live on the lands which are around The Blue Smoke Mountains.

At this time, the animals of the world still talked to men and taught them how to live on and care for the land. These people were called "The One True People". In this tribe lived a brave warrior woman.

She was called Arrow Woman. Arrow Woman was taught to use the bow, the spear and the knife. Even though it was a warrior's job to hunt and fight, Arrow Woman could shoot straighter with the bow than any warrior, she could throw the knife so it split a branch no bigger than your thumb and she could throw the spear into eye of a hawk in flight.

Because of all this, no warrior would tell her to be like a woman.

One day while on a hunt, Arrow Woman came upon the tracks of Yona the Bear. She saw blood on the ground and knew him to be wounded so she followed his tracks. High into the mountains she followed. Soon she came to a place that she did not know. It was in this place, a place known only to the animals that she finally saw Yona the Bear. He had a deep cut in his side and she saw him bowing down in prayer. She saw him bowing toward a large field of tall grass and speaking words that she had not heard before. Suddenly, the grass shimmered and became a lake. Arrow Woman saw Yona the Bear dive into the water. After a time, he emerged from the water, his side was completely healed. Yona the Bear then saw Arrow Woman and walked to her. Yona the Bear told her, "This is the sacred lake of the animals. It is called, 'Atagahi' and its location is known only to the animals. It is where we come for healing and strength. You are the first man creature to see the sacred lake.

You must never tell your kind of its location for it is the home of 'The Great Uktena'. With these words Yona the Bear turned and walked into the woods and disappeared.

Arrow Woman was tired after following Yona the Bear all day so she decided to rest a while by this lake. She built a small fire and sat down to eat a meal that she had brought with her. She took a drink of the water from the lake and felt instantly refreshed. She was amazed, she felt strong as the Buffalo. She felt as if she run faster than the Raven could fly.

The woods were quiet, the Wind was sleeping, the Sun was shining bright but was not hot, the surface of the lake was completely calm, Arrow Woman began to get sleepy.

It was at this time that she saw Uktena, she had been told of him when she was a child but no one in her tribe ever claimed to have seen him. High above the water he raised his great serpent's head, the jewel in his forehead glistening.

He began to move toward her. Arrow Woman grabbed up her spear and stood up to face the great creature coming to her, standing proud, showing no fear, the way any warrior should. She raised her spear and prepared to strike the huge beast.

Uktena stopped a short distance from her. He smiled; his mouth was larger than a man was tall and full of teeth longer than man's forearm. He spoke to Arrow Woman on the bank of his lake. To her he said, "Put down your weapons for I mean you no harm. I come only to teach."

Arrow Woman laid down her spear and began to relax, somehow knowing Uktena spoke truly.

Uktena told her to sit and to listen. Uktena dipped his head below the surface and came back up a moment later. In his mouth he had a strangely crooked stick and a leather pouch. These things he laid on the ground in front of Arrow Woman. Then the Great Uktena began to teach her. He said, "This that I have laid before you is the Sacred Pipe of The Creator." He then told her to pick up the pipe." The bowl is of the same red clay The Creator used to make your kind. The red clay is Woman kind and is from the Earth. Just as a woman bears the children and brings forth life, the bowl bears the sacred tobacco and brings forth smoke. The stem is Man. Rigid and strong the stem is from the plant kingdom and like a man it supports the bowl just as man supports his family."

Uktena then showed Arrow Woman how to join the bowl to the stem saying, "Just as a man and a woman remain separate until joined in marriage so too are the bowl and stem separate. Never to be joined unless the pipe is used."

Uktena then showed her how place the sacred tobacco into the pipe and with an ember from the fire lit the tobacco so it burned slightly.

He told her this, "The smoke is the breath of The Creator, when you draw the smoke into your body, you will be cleansed and made whole. When the smoke leaves your mouth, it will rise to The Creator. Your prayers, your dreams, your hopes and desires will be taken to Him in the smoke. Also, the truth in your soul will be shown to Him when you smoke the pipe. If you are not true, do not smoke the pipe. If your spirit is bad and you seek to deceive, do not smoke the pipe."

Uktena continued his lesson well into the night teaching Arrow Woman all of the prayers used with the pipe and all of the reasons for using the pipe. He finished just as the Moon was beginning her nightly journey across the sky in search of her true love. He told Arrow Woman to wrap the pipe in cloth, keeping the parts separate. With this done, he told her that she would never again be able to find this place but to remember all that she had learned. Uktena then returned to depths of the lake. Arrow Woman saw the water shimmer and become again the field of grass.

She left, taking with her the pipe and her lessons and a wondrous tale.

Ever since that time, The Indians have used the sacred pipe and never again has any man seen the sacred lake of Uktena.

THE ORIGIN OF FIRE

(Cherokee)

Long, long ago, animals and trees talked with each other, but there was no fire at that time. Fox was most clever and he tried to think of a way to create fire for the world.

One day, he decided to visit the Geese, to learn how to imitate. They agreed to teach him if he would fly with them. So, they fixed a way to attach wings to Fox, but cautioned him never to open his eyes while flying.

Whenever the Geese arose in flight, Fox also flew along with them to practice their cry. On one such adventure, darkness descended suddenly as they flew over the village of the fireflies. In midflight, the glare from the flickering fireflies caused Fox to forget and he opened his eyes, instantly his wings collapsed! His fall was uncontrollable. He landed within the walled area of the firefly village, where a fire constantly burned in the center.

Two kind Fireflies came to see the fallen Fox, who gave each one a necklace of juniper berries.

Fox hoped to persuade the two Fireflies to tell him where he could find a way over the wall to the outside. They led him to a cedar tree, which they explained would bend down upon command and throw him over the wall if he so desired.

That evening, Fox found the spring where Fireflies obtained their water. There also, he discovered colored Earth, which when mixed with water made paint. He decided to give himself a coat of white. Upon returning to the village, Fox suggested to the Fireflies, “Let’s have a festival where we can dance and I will produce the music.”

They all agreed that would be fun and helped to gather wood to build up a greater fire. Secretly, Fox tied a piece of cedar bark to his tail. Then he made a drum, probably the first one ever constructed, and beat it forcefully with a stick for the dancing Fireflies. Gradually, he moved closer and closer to the fire.

Fox pretended to tire out from beating the drum. He gave it to some Fireflies who wanted to help make the music. Fox quickly thrust his tail into the fire, lighting the bark, and exclaimed, "It is too warm here for me, I must find a cooler place."

Straight to the cedar tree Fox ran, calling, "Bend down to me, my cedar tree, bend down!"

Down bent the cedar tree for Fox to catch hold, then up it carried him far over the wall. On and on he ran, with the Fireflies in pursuit.

As Fox ran, brush and wood on either side of his path were ignited from the sparks dropping from the burning bark tied to his tail.

Fox finally tired and gave the burning bark to Hawk, who carried it to Brown Crane. He flew far southward, scattering fire sparks everywhere. This is how fire first spread over the Earth.

Fireflies continued chasing Fox all the way to his burrow and declared, "Forever after, Wily Fox, your punishment for stealing our fire will be that you can never make use of it for yourself."

HOW THE MILKY WAY CAME TO BE

(Cherokee)

One morning an older man and his wife went to their storage basket for some cornmeal. They discovered that someone or something had gotten into the cornmeal during the night. This upset them very much for no one in a Cherokee village stole from someone else.

Then they noticed that the cornmeal was scattered over the ground. In the middle of the meal were giant dog prints. These dog prints were so large that the elderly Indians knew this was no ordinary dog.

They immediately alerted the people of the village. It was decided that this must be a spirit dog from another world. The people did not want the spirit dog coming to their village. They decided to get rid of the spirit dog by frightening it so badly it would never return. They gathered their drums and turtle shell rattles and later that night they hid around the area where the cornmeal was kept.

Late into the night they heard a whirring sound like many bird wings. They looked up to see the form of a giant dog swooping down from the sky. It landed near the basket and then began to eat great mouthfuls of cornmeal.

Suddenly the natives jumped up shouting and beating and shaking their noise makers. The noise was so loud it sounded like thunder. The giant dog turned and began to run down the path. The natives chased after him making the loudest noises they could. The giant dog ran to the top of a hill and leaped into the sky, the cornmeal spilling out the sides of its mouth.

The giant dog ran across the black night sky until it disappeared from sight. But the cornmeal that had spilled from its mouth made a path way across the sky. Each grain of cornmeal became a star. The Cherokees call that pattern of stars, "the place where the dog ran."

WHAT THE STARS ARE LIKE

(Cherokee)

One night a hunting party camping in the mountains noticed two lights like large stars moving along the top of a distant ridge. They wondered and watched until the light disappeared on the other side. The next night, and the next, they saw the lights again moving along the distant ridge, and after talking over the matter they decided to go and try to learn the cause. In the morning they started out and went until they came to the distant ridge, where, after searching some time, they found two strange creatures, with round bodies covered with fine fur or downy feathers, from which small heads stuck out like the heads of Terrapins. As the breeze played upon these feathers showers of sparks flew out.

The hunters carried the strange creatures back to the camp, intending to take them home to the settlements on their return. They kept them several days and noticed that every night they would grow bright and shine like great stars, although by day they were only balls of gray fur, except when the wind stirred and made the sparks fly out. They kept very quiet, and no one thought of their trying to escape, when, on the seventh night, the creatures suddenly rose from the ground like balls of fire and were soon above the tops of the trees. Higher and higher they went, while the wondering hunters watched, until at last they were only two bright points of light in the dark sky, and then the hunters knew that they were stars.

BUFFALO WOMAN

(Caddo)

Snow Bird, the Caddo Medicine Man, had a handsome son. When the boy was old enough to be given a man's name, Snow Bird called him Braveness because of his courage as a hunter. Many of the girls in the Caddo village wanted to win Braveness as a husband, but he paid little attention to any of them.

One morning Braveness started out for a day of hunting, and while he was walking along looking for game, he saw someone ahead of him sitting under a small elm tree. As he approached, he was surprised to find that the person was a young woman, and he started to turn aside.

"Come here," she called to him in a pleasant voice.

Braveness went up to her and saw that she was very young and very beautiful.

"I knew you were coming here," she said, "and so I came to meet you."

"You are not of my people," Braveness replied. "How did you know that I was coming this way?"

"I am Buffalo Woman," she said. "I have seen you many times before, from afar. I want you to take me home with you and let me stay with you."

"I can take you home with me," Braveness answered her, "but you must ask my parents if you can stay with us."

They started for his home at once, and when they arrived there Buffalo Woman asked Braveness's parents if she could stay with them and become the young man's wife.

"If Braveness wants you for his wife, we will be pleased," said Snow Bird, the Medicine Man. "It is time that he had someone to love."

And so, Braveness and Buffalo Woman were married in the custom of the Caddo people and lived happily together for several moons.

One day she asked him, "Will you do whatever I may ask of you, Braveness?"

"Yes," Braveness replied, "if what you ask is not unreasonable."

"I want you to go with me to visit my people."

Braveness said that he would go, and the next day they started for her home, she leading the way. After they had walked a long distance they came to some high hills and all at once she turned round and looked at Braveness and said, "You promised me that you would do anything I say."

"Yes," he answered.

"Well," she said, "my home is on the other side of this high hill. I will tell you when we get to my mother. I know there will be many coming there to see who you are, and some may aggravate you and try to make you angry, but do not allow yourself to become angry with any of them. Some may try to kill you."

"Why should they do that?" asked Braveness.

"Listen to what I am about to tell you," she said. "I knew you before you knew me. Through magic, I made you come to me that first day. I said that some will try to make you angry, and if you show anger at even one of them, the others will join in fighting you until they have killed you. They will be jealous of you. The reason is that I refused many who wanted me."

"But you are now my wife," Braveness said.

"I have told you what to do when we get there," Buffalo Woman continued. "Now I want you to lie down on the ground and roll over twice."

Braveness smiled at her, but he did as she had told him to do. He rolled over twice, and when he stood up, he found himself changed into a Buffalo.

For a moment Buffalo Woman looked at him, seeing the astonishment in his eyes. Then she rolled over twice, and she also became a Buffalo. Without saying a word, she led him to the top of the hill. In the valley off to the West, Braveness could see hundreds and hundreds of Buffalo.

"They are my people," said Buffalo Woman. "This is my home."

When the members of the nearest herd saw Braveness and Buffalo Woman coming, they began gathering in one place, as though waiting for them. Buffalo Woman led the way, Braveness following her until they reached an old Buffalo Cow, and he knew that she was the mother of his beautiful wife.

For two moons they stayed with the herd. Every now and then, four or five of the young Buffalo Bulls would come around and annoy Braveness, trying to arouse his anger, but he pretended not to notice them. One night, Buffalo Woman told him that she was ready to go back to his home, and they slipped away over the hills.

When they reached the place where they had turned themselves into Buffalo, they rolled over twice on the ground and became a man and a woman again.

"Promise me that you will not tell anyone of this magical transformation," Buffalo Woman said. "If people learn about it, something bad will happen to us."

They stayed at Braveness's home for twelve moons, and then Buffalo Woman asked him again to go with her to visit her people. They had not been long in the valley of the Buffalo when she told Braveness that the young Buffalo Bulls who were jealous of him were planning to have a race. "They will challenge you to race and if you do not outrun them, they will kill you," she said.

That night Braveness could not sleep. He went out to take a long walk. It was a very dark night without moon or stars, but he could feel the presence of the Wind spirit.

"You are young and strong," the Wind spirit whispered to him, "but you cannot outrun the Buffalo without my help. If you lose, they will kill you. If you win, they will never challenge you again.

"What must I do to save my life and keep my beautiful wife?" asked Braveness.

The Wind spirit gave him two things. "One of these is a magic herb," said the Wind spirit. "The other is dried mud from a medicine wallow. If the Buffalo catch up with you, first throw behind you the magic herb. If they come too close to you again, throw down the dried mud."

The next day was the day of the race. At sunrise the young Buffalo gathered at the starting place. When Braveness joined them, they began making fun of him, telling him he was a man Buffalo and therefore had not the power to outrun them. Braveness ignored their jeers, and calmly lined up with them at the starting point.

An old Buffalo started the race with a loud bellow, and at first Braveness took the lead, running very swiftly. But soon the others began gaining on him, and when he heard their hard breathing close upon his heels, he threw the magic herb behind him. By this time, he was growing very tired and thought he could not run any more. He looked back and saw one Buffalo Bull holding his head down and coming very fast, rapidly closing the space between him and Braveness. Just as this Buffalo was about to catch up with him, Braveness threw down the dried mud from the medicine wallow.

Soon he was far ahead again, but he knew that he had used up the powers given him by the Wind spirit. As he neared the goal set for the race, he heard the pounding of hooves coming closer behind him. At the last moment, he felt a strong wind on his face as it passed him to stir up dust and keep the Buffalo from overtaking him. With the help of the Wind spirit, Braveness crossed the goal first and won the race. After that, none of the Buffalo ever challenged him again, and he and Buffalo Woman lived peacefully with the herd until they were ready to return to his Caddo people.

Not long after their return to Braveness's home, Buffalo Woman gave birth to a handsome son. They named him Buffalo Boy, and soon he was old enough to play with the other children of the village. One day while Buffalo Woman was cooking dinner, Buffalo Boy slipped out of the lodge and went to join some other children at play. They played several games and then decided to play that they were Buffalo. Some of them lay on the ground to roll like Buffalo, and Buffalo Boy also did this. When Buffalo Boy rolled over twice, he changed into a real Buffalo Calf. Frightened by this, the other children ran for their lodges.

About this time his mother came out to look for him, and when she saw the children running in fear, she knew that something must be wrong. She went to see what had happened and found her son changed into a Buffalo Calf. Taking him up in her arms, she ran down the hill, and as soon as she was out of sight of the village, she turned herself into a Buffalo and with Buffalo Boy started off toward the West.

Later that evening when Braveness returned from hunting, he could find neither his wife nor his son in the lodge. He went out to look for them, and someone told him of the game the children had played and of the magic that had changed his son into a Buffalo Calf.

At first, Braveness could not believe what they told him, but after he had followed his wife's tracks down the hill and found the place where she had rolled, he knew the story was true. For many moons, Braveness searched for Buffalo Woman and Buffalo Boy, but he never found them again.

COYOTE AND TURTLE RUN A RACE

(Caddo)

One time, as Coyote was returning from a long and unsuccessful hunt for food, he passed the home of his old friend Turtle. Being weary and hungry and in no hurry, he decided to stop and make Turtle a visit. Turtle invited him in and offered him something to eat, as Coyote had hoped that he would.

While Coyote ate, Turtle stretched himself out to rest, saying, "I am tired out. I have just come back from the races."

Coyote asked "What races?"

"Our people have been having foot races down by the river. Have you not heard of them?" answered Turtle.

Coyote smiled at the thought of Turtle's racing and said that he had not heard of the races, and if he had he surely would have been there.

"Who won?" he asked.

"I did," said Turtle. "I have never yet been beaten in a race with my people."

Coyote answered, "I have never been beaten either. I wonder how a race between us would come out."

"The way to find out is to have a race," Turtle said.

"I am willing, if you are. When shall we have it?" Coyote answered. They determined to run the race two days hence. In the meantime, Coyote had finished eating, and so, promising to come on the second day to run the race, he departed.

When he arrived home, Coyote sent his son to call all of the Coyote people and announce to them that his father was going to run a race with Turtle, and that he wanted them all to come and bet heavily on the race, for of course he would defeat Turtle.

As soon as Coyote had gone Turtle sent his son out to announce that his father was going to run a race with Coyote, and that he wanted all of the best runners to come to his lodge. They all came and listened to Turtle's plan to beat Coyote in the race.

Turtle arose when they came in and said, "We all know that Coyote is a good runner, but he is also a cheat. He has cheated us in many ways. Let us now cheat him out of this race. Will you help me do it?"

Every one present agreed to help him.

Then Turtle continued, "This is my plan. I want each one of you to put a white feather in your hair just like the one I wear, and paint yourselves to look just like me. Then station yourselves at intervals along the course. Coyote will run with his head down, as he always does. One of you will start with him, but when he has left you far behind drop down in the grass. Then the next one will jump up and run. Coyote will look up and see you ahead, and then he will run until he passes you. Then the next one will jump up and run, and so on until the last one. I will be the last, and beat him over the goal."

The Turtles talked over the plan, then arose and went home to prepare for the race.

The first day passed, and then the day came when they had to run the race. Early in the morning the Turtles stationed themselves along the way in the tall grass, and soon Coyote came. They began to discuss the distance they should run. Turtle wanted to run a long distance, but Coyote did not want to go a very long distance; he thought that he could beat Turtle in a short distance just as easily as in a long distance, and he did not care to tire himself. Turtle insisted, and so Coyote said that he would agree to any distance that he would mention. Many Coyotes came and began to bet on Coyote.

Coyote and Turtle started to run and all the Coyotes began to laugh, for their Coyote was far ahead, but soon to their surprise, Turtle was ahead. Coyote overtook Turtle, and then they began to laugh again. Soon they heard the Turtles cheering, and to their amazement, Turtle was far in the lead. Again, Coyote overtook Turtle, and again Turtle came up far in the lead. The Coyotes cheered one moment and the Turtles the next. Just as Coyote had passed Turtle and was near the goal, Turtle crossed the line, and all the Turtles set up a loud cheer.

Coyote ran off in the grass, and is wondering yet how Turtle beat him in the race, and all the other Coyotes are angry at him because he lost the race and caused them to lose so many bets.

EVENING STAR AND ORPHAN STAR

(Caddo)

A poor orphan boy lived with a large family of natives who were not kind to him and mistreated him. He could not go to play or hunt with the other boys, but had to do all of the hard work. Whenever the camp moved the family always tried to leave the boy behind, but sooner or later he found their new camp and went to them because he had no other place to go.

One time several families went in boats to an island in a large lake to hunt eggs, and the orphan boy went with them. After they had filled their boats with eggs, they secretly made ready to go back to the mainland. In the night, while the orphan boy was asleep, they stole away in their boats, leaving him to starve on the lonely island.

The boy wandered about the island, eating only the scraps that he could find around the dead camp fires, until he was almost starved. As he did not have a bow and arrows, he could not hunt, but he sat by the water's edge and tried to catch fish as they swam past him.

One day as he sat on the lonely shore, he saw a large animal with horns coming to him through the water. He sat very still and watched the animal, for he was too frightened to run away.

The monster came straight to him, then raised his head out of the water and said, "Boy, I have come to save you. I saw the people desert you and I have taken pity upon you and come to save you. Get upon my back and hold to my horns and I will carry you to the mainland."

The boy was no longer afraid, but climbed upon the animal's back.

"Keep your eyes on the blue sky, and if you see a star tell me at once," the animal said to him.

They had not gone far when the boy cried, "There in the West is a big star."

The monster looked up and saw the star, then turned around at once and swam back to the island as fast as he could. The next day he came and took the boy again, telling him, as before, to call out the moment that he saw a star appear in the sky.

They had gone a little farther than they had the day before when the boy cried out, "There in the West is a star."

The animal turned around and went to the shore. The next day and the next four days he started with the boy, and each time he succeeded in getting a little farther before the boy saw the star.

The sixth time they were within a few feet of the opposite shore when the boy saw the star. He wanted to reach the shore so badly that he thought he would keep still and not tell the monster that he saw the star, for he knew that he would take him back to the island at once if he did.

He said nothing, and so the monster swam on until they were almost in shallow water, when the boy saw a great black cloud roll in front of the star. He became frightened and jumped off of the animal's back and swam to the shore. Just as he jumped something struck the animal with an awful crash and he rolled over dead.

When the boy came upon the shore a handsome young Warrior came up to him and said, "You have done me a great favor. For a long time, I have tried to kill this monster, because he makes the water of the lake dangerous, but until now I could never get the chance. In return for what you have done, I will take you with me to the sky, if you care to go."

The boy said that he wanted to go, as he was alone and friendless upon the earth. The man, who was Evening Star, took him with him to the sky, and there he may be seen as Orphan Star who stands near Evening Star.

RED SHIELD AND RUNNING WOLF

(Crow)

For many years the Sioux and the Crows were enemies. The tribes were not friends and never married each other.

Red Shield first heard of Running Wolf from a Sioux woman who had been captured by the Crows and then later was permitted to return to her people. This woman had lived as a prisoner with Running Wolf's family during the time when the boy was growing up.

"He was a lazy boy," the Sioux woman told Red Shield. "His father had to drive him out of bed every morning by rapping his shins with a stick. One morning he scolded the boy very hard and told him that he should be out hunting deer for the family. That morning, as soon as the father left the teepee, Running Wolf came to me and asked if I would make a buckskin mask for him. And so, I made him a mask, and he spent the day painting it with white clay and fastening Deer horns to it. Before sunrise the next morning he was the first one out of bed. He took his father's gun and knife and rode away on a horse, with two led horses behind him. He went out to a little lake near their village, fastened his horses in the woods, and then went down to a place where animals come to drink. When the Sun rose some Deer came there, but they did not run away because they thought the boy was a Deer. He killed two Deer, loaded them on the led horses, and brought them home just as his father was waking up."

"Was Running Wolf's father pleased by this?" Red Shield asked.

"Oh, yes. He told his son that he had done well, and should divide the venison with their neighbors. But that was not the end of it. The next morning the boy went back to the watering place and returned with two more Deer, and the morning after that he did the same."

The Sioux woman smiled. "That time his father told him to stop or he would begin to smell like a Deer."

"And what did young Running Wolf say to this?" Red Shield asked.

"He said nothing, but he began sleeping late again, until one morning his father rapped him on the legs and scolded him for being lazy. His father told Running Wolf that he could no longer use the family's horses, that if he wanted a horse to ride, he would have to go out and take one from the Nez Perces.

That morning, as soon as his father went hunting, Running Wolf came to me and asked if I would make him a new pair of moccasins. I did this for him, and he spent the day decorating them with paint and beads in some special way. At sundown, he left the teepee with his gun, not saying a word to anyone. Next morning, he returned with twenty horses that he had taken from the Nez Perces."

"His father must have been much pleased by this," said Red Shield.

"Oh, yes, after the boy gave him ten of the horses, the father sang praise songs for him all day. But that was not the end of it. That night Running Wolf went out again, and next morning he brought back forty horses and gave them all to his father. And the next night he captured fifty horses, all of which he gave to his father. And still a fourth night he went and this time he brought back eighty head of horses, giving them all to his father! Oh, I can tell you, Running Wolf's father had a hard time herding all those horses.

'Stop! Stop!' he shouted at his son. 'You have listened too well to what I told you."

Red Shield laughed. "I think I like this young Running Wolf, even if he is a Crow," she said.

"Oh, but he soon grew up after that," the Sioux woman said. "After his father died, his mother and I made a new teepee for him, and then I was told that I could return to my tribe. Running Wolf painted his teepee black, tied feathers to the door, and laid war bonnets and other finery around the inside to signify that he intended to become a mighty warrior."

Not long after Red Shield heard these stories about Running Wolf, her father announced that the Sioux would be going out for their summer Buffalo hunt. The tribe camped in a narrow valley down which some of their hunters would drive the Buffalo while others waited in concealment on either side to kill them as they passed. It was a busy time for Red Shield and the other women, young and old, for they helped in the skinning of the Buffalo and then stretched the hides out to dry in the sun.

One afternoon while half the Sioux hunters were out searching for a Buffalo herd, an alarm suddenly spread through the camp. "Crow horse thieves are coming! Look to the horses!"

As soon as the men drove the horses in, it was the duty of the women and children to guard them while the warriors went out to protect the camp from the Crow raid.

Red Shield mounted her spotted pony and joined the other women. Far up the level valley she could see the dust of the oncoming Crows as they raced toward the line of defending Sioux. A moment later she heard the sharp war cries of the contending warriors.

She saw one of the Crow warriors on a black horse break through the Sioux line and come charging toward the horse herd she was helping to guard. Not far behind him, two Sioux warriors galloped in pursuit. As the Crow came nearer, she could see that he wore four eagle feathers in his hair. Fastened behind his belt was a streamer of black leather long enough to trail on the ground. His horse's mane and tail were whitened with clay. He carried a black handled spear decorated with bunches of Crow feathers, and this weapon was pointed straight at Red Shield. She held her spotted horse steady, defying the Crow, and at the last moment he reined in the black horse so that the point of the spear was only an arm's length from her body.

The young Crow's face was painted with streaks of black and white. For a moment he glared at Red Shield, his eyes very bright, and then he threw back his head and laughed. By this time his pursuers had caught up with him. One of the Sioux put an arrow to his bow but missed; then both of them closed in upon the Crow with their war clubs raised, ready to strike.

Dancing his black horse in a circle, the Crow used his spear to knock first one and then the other Sioux off their horses. His horse pawed the earth, and then sprang like a cat into the Sioux horse herd. Before Red Shield or her companions could move, the Crow had cut six horses out of their herd and was chasing them off down the valley.

Angry and frustrated because she could do nothing to stop the daring Crow, Red Shield watched him go. Then the young man turned and waved a farewell to her. Above the pounding hooves she could hear his laughter, and her annoyance turned to unwilling admiration.

A group of Sioux warriors swept by intent upon pursuit, but Red Shield's father called them back. "Too many of our hunters are away," he said. "We are too few to risk leaving our women and children and the horse herd open to another raid."

"Did you see that Crow!" cried an old Sioux Medicine Man. "He and his horse are under some powerful magic."

The Sioux woman who had once been a captive among the Crows spoke up from the front of her teepee. "I know that one," she said.

"What name does he go by?" the Medicine Man asked.

"Yes, who is he?" demanded Red Shield's father.

"Running Wolf, he is called." The Sioux woman who had once been a captive among the Crows answered.

Red Shield, who still sat on her spotted horse, whispered to herself: "Running Wolf! I knew he must be Running Wolf"

Not long after that the Sioux returned to their village on the Missouri River. It seemed to all the young men in the tribe that the Chief's daughter, Red Shield, had suddenly become a great beauty, and one by one they came by the

Chief's teepee to ask if she would marry them. Red Shield's father encouraged her to choose one of the suitors for a husband, but she wanted none of them. One evening after she had rejected a handsome young warrior, her father demanded to know why she was so stubborn.

"Because I do not love him!" she cried, and in a fit of anger she threw her supper into the fire.

"If you love someone else," her father said patiently, "then tell me his name."

"I love only Running Wolf," she replied. "I want to marry him."

"You cannot marry Running Wolf! He is a Crow, and the Crows are our enemies."

Her father thought that would put an end to it, but days passed without Red Shield saying a word, and she ate so little that she began to grow thin. At last he realized that his daughter was determined to marry Running Wolf or else will herself to die.

"Very well," the Chief said, "at least you are a woman of courage. You do not know if Running Wolf wants you for a wife, but you are determined to test him."

The next morning the Chief brought around two fine horses, a mule, and some packs filled with moccasins and other presents. He summoned the Sioux woman who had once been a captive of the Crows and told her to go with Red Shield until they found the Crow camp where Running Wolf lived. They started out and at the end of three days they sighted the Crow teepees along a little stream. They rode into a thick wood where they fastened their horses and the pack mule. Red Shield painted herself carefully and dressed in her best clothing. By this time night had fallen, but a full moon was rising above the trees.

"It's time for me to go into the Crow camp," Red Shield said.

"Remember to look for a black teepee," the Sioux woman reminded her. "You will see a bunch of eagle feathers fastened to the end of one of the poles."

“If I don’t return,” Red Shield whispered, “you will know that Running Wolf does not want me for a wife and that I am a prisoner of the Crows as you once were.”

“I will wait for you,” the Sioux woman said.

Red Shield walked out of the woods and entered the bright moonlight which flooded the Crow camp. In the middle of the camp she found a black teepee with eagle feathers fastened to the top of one of the poles. No one noticed her as she walked to the teepee.

Inside some young men were talking and smoking around a campfire. Red Shield was certain that one of them was Running Wolf. She sat down outside the entrance. After a while the young men began to leave, one or two at a time, paying no particular attention to her presence.

Then Running Wolf came out to stretch himself and yawn.

The moonlight was full on his face, and Red Shield felt her heart beat strongly.

He saw her then, and said in Crow, “Come in,” but Red Shield understood not one word of Crow and she didn’t answer him or moved.

Running Wolf shrugged and went back inside, and Red Shield heard him say something else. The voice of an old woman responded.

Red Shield arose then and went into the teepee. The fire had died to a few coals and she could see only the shadowy forms of Running Wolf and his mother. She went close to the fire and sat down as though to warm herself.

This time the old woman spoke to her in Crow. “Take off your moccasins and rest.” But of course, Red Shield did not understand.

“Build up the fire so that we can see this young woman,” said Running Wolf. His mother placed some dry wood on the coals, and a blaze sprang up to light the inside of the teepee.

“This is not a Crow woman!” cried Running Wolf’s mother.

"No," he said. "But I know who she is. Only one time have I seen her but her face has been in my dreams many times since. She is Sioux."

Red Shield raised her head, and made signs to tell them she could not understand what they were saying, but that she had a friend nearby who could speak for her. At last Running Wolf understood, and he followed her across the camp clearing into the thick woods where the Sioux woman was waiting with the horses and pack mule. Running Wolf remembered the former prisoner of his boyhood, and when they returned to his teepee the Sioux woman and his mother had a happy reunion.

"Why do you and this daughter of a Sioux chief come into our camp?" the mother asked.

"She is Red Shield," replied the Sioux woman. "She has brought many presents. She has come to marry your son, Running Wolf"

"And what does my son, Running Wolf, have to say to this? To marry one of the enemies?"

Running Wolf looked at Red Shield. "I knew she was beautiful, and she showed courage that day I took horses from the Sioux. Now she has shown more bravery than I would have dared, by coming into the camp of her enemies alone. I want her for my wife. "

While the Sioux woman was bringing in the packs of presents, Running Wolf's mother went through the camp. "Come and look at my son's wife!" she cried. "One of the enemy's children has come to marry him!"

All the Crows in camp came to see Red Shield, and all said she was very good looking and a young woman of great bravery.

Early the next morning the Sioux woman started back on the long journey to the Missouri River to tell the girl's father that she was safe and was now the wife of the Crow warrior, Running Wolf.

A few days later Red Shield's father, the Sioux Chief, sent two messengers to the Crow Chief, telling him that he and many of his relatives were coming to pay the Crows a friendly visit.

For this event the Crows moved their teepees to a larger plain beside a lake, camping in a tight circle so as to leave room for the visitors. The Crow Chief told Running Wolf to put his black teepee in the place of honor in the center. When the Sioux arrived, the Crows surrounded them and watched them put up their teepees. After this was done, Red Shield took Running Wolf to welcome her parents, and they all exchanged many presents. Running Wolf brought several guns and the horses he had taken from the Sioux and gave them to Red Shield's father.

For four days and nights the Sioux camped with the Crows and the tribes danced together every evening. After the Sioux returned to the Missouri River, Running Wolf and Red Shield and several of their friends visited them from time to time, and in the moons of pleasant weather, her Sioux father and mother came to visit their daughter, and later on to see their grandchildren. In both tribes, the young Crow warrior and his Sioux wife were regarded as hero and heroine, and their people lived in peace for a very long time.

LODGE BOY AND THROWN AWAY

(Crow)

Once upon a time there lived a couple, the woman was pregnant. The man went hunting one day, and in his absence a certain wicked woman named Red Woman came to the teepee and killed his wife and cut her open and found boy twins.

She threw one behind the teepee curtain, and the other she threw into a spring. She then put a stick inside the woman and stuck one end in the ground, to give her the form of a live person, and burned her upper lip, giving her the appearance as though laughing.

When her husband came home, tired from carrying the deer he had killed, he saw his wife standing near the door of the teepee, looking as though she were laughing at him, and he said: "I am tired and hungry, why do you laugh at me?" and pushed her. As she fell backwards, her stomach opened, and he caught hold of her and discovered she was dead. He knew at once that Red Woman had killed his wife.

While the man was eating supper alone one night a voice said, "Father, give me some of your supper." As no one was in sight, he resumed eating and again the voice asked for supper.

The man said, "Whoever you are, come and eat with me, for I am poor and alone."

A young boy came from behind the curtain, and said his name was "Thrown Behind the Curtain." During the day, while the man went hunting, the boy stayed home.

One day the boy said, "Father, make me two bows and the arrows."

His father asked him why he wanted two bows.

The boy said, "I want them to use with hunting different animals."

His father made them for him, but guessed the boy had other reasons, and decided he would watch the boy, and on one day, earlier than usual, he left his teepee and hid upon a hill overlooking his teepee, and while there, he saw two boys of about the same age shooting arrows.

That evening when he returned home, he asked his son, "Is there not another little boy of your age about here?"

His son said, "Yes, and he lives in the spring."

His father said, "You should bring him out and make him live with us."

The son said, "I cannot make him, because he has sharp teeth like an otter, but if you will make me a suit of rawhide, I will try and catch him."

One day, arrangements were made to catch the boy.

The father said, "I will stay here in the teepee and you tell him I have gone out."

So, Thrown Behind The Curtain said to Thrown In Spring, "Come out and play arrows."

Thrown In Spring came out just a little, and said, "I smell something."

Thrown Behind The Curtain said, "No, you don't, my father is not home," and after insisting, Thrown In Spring came out, and both boys began to play. While they were playing, Thrown Behind The Curtain disagreed with a point of their game, and as Thrown In Spring stooped over to see how close his arrow came, Thrown Behind The Curtain grabbed him from behind and held his arms close to his sides and Thrown In Spring turned and tried to bite him, but his teeth could not break through the rawhide suit.

The father came to help Thrown Behind The Curtain and the water of the spring rushed out to help Thrown In Spring; but Thrown In Spring was dragged to a high hill where the water could not reach him, and there they burned incense under his nose, and he became human. The three of them lived together.

One day one of the boys said, "Let us go and wake up mother."

They went to the mother's grave and Thrown Behind The Curtain said, "Mother, your stone pot is dropping," and she moved.

Thrown In Spring said, "Mother, your hide dresser is falling," and she sat up.

Then Thrown Behind The Curtain of them said, "Mother, your bone crusher is falling," and she began to arrange her hair, which had begun to fall off.

The mother said, "I have been asleep a long time." The she went home with the boys.

The boy's father did not allowed them to go to the river bend above their teepee; for an old woman lived there who had a boiling pot, and every time she saw any living object, she tilted the kettle toward it and the object was drawn into the pot and boiled for her to eat.

The boys went one day to see the old woman, and they found her asleep and they stole up and got her pot and awakened the old woman and said to her, "Grandmother, why have you this here?" at the same time tilting the pot towards her, by which she was drowned and boiled to death. They took the pot home and gave it to their mother for her own protection.

Their father told them not to disobey him again and said, "There is something over the hill I do not want you to go near."

They were very anxious to find out what this thing was, and they went over to the hill and as they poked their heads over the hilltop, the thing began to draw in air, and the boys were drawn in also; and as they went in, they saw dead or dying people and animals. The thing proved to be an immense alligator like serpent.

One of the boys touched the kidneys of the thing and asked what they were. The alligator like serpent said, "That is my medicine, do not touch it.

The boy reached up and touched its heart and asked what it was, and the alligator like serpent grunted and said, "This is where I make my plans."

One of the boys said, “You do make plans, do you?” and he cut the heart off and it died. They made their escape by cutting between the ribs and freed the living ones and took a piece of the heart home to their father.

After the father had administered another scolding, he told the boys not to go near the three trees standing in a triangular shaped piece of ground; for if anything went under them they would bend to the ground suddenly, killing everything in their way. One day the boys went towards these trees, running swiftly and then stopping suddenly near the trees, which bent violently and struck the ground without hitting them. They jumped over the trees, breaking the branches and they could not rise after the branches were broken.

Once more the boys were scolded and told not to go near a teepee over the hill; for it was inhabited by snakes, and they would approach anyone asleep and enter his body through their bottom. Again, the boys did as they were told not to do and went to the teepee, and the snakes invited them in. They went in and carried flat pieces of stone with them and as they sat down they placed the flat pieces of stones under their bottoms.

After they had been in the teepee a short while, the snakes began putting their heads over the poles around the fireplace and the snakes began to relate stories, and one of them said “When there is a drizzling rain, and when we are under cover, it is nice to sleep.”

One of the boys said, “When we are lying down under the pine trees and the wind blows softly through them and has a weird sound, it is nice to sleep.”

All but one of the snakes went to sleep, and that one tried to bite the bottom of each of the boys and failed, on account of the flat stone. The boys killed all of the other snakes but that one, and they took that one and rubbed its head against the side of a cliff, and that is the reason why snakes have flattened heads.

Again the boys were scolded by their father, who said, "There is a man living on the steep cut bank, with deep water under it, and if you go near it he will push you over the bank into the water for his father in the water to eat."

The boys went to the place, but before leaving, they fixed their headdresses with dried grass.

Upon their arrival at the edge of the bank, one boy said to the other boy, "Just as he is about to push you over, lie down quickly."

The man from his hiding place suddenly rushed out to push the boys over, and just as he was about to do it, the boys threw themselves quickly on the ground, and the man went over their heads, pulling their headdress with him, and his father in the water ate him.

Upon the boys' return, and after telling what they had done, their father scolded them and told them, "There is a man who wears moccasins of fire, and when he wants anything, he goes around it and it is burned up."

The boys traveled to where this man lived and stole upon him one day when he was sleeping under a tree and each one of the boys took off a moccasin and put it on and they awoke him and ran about him and he was burned and went up in smoke. They took the moccasins home.

Their father told them that something would yet happen to them; for they had killed so many bad things. One day while walking in the valley they were lifted from the earth and after traveling in mid air for some time, they were placed on top of a peak in a rough high mountain with a big lake surrounding it and the Thunder Bird said to them, "I want you to kill a long Otter that lives in the lake; he eats all the young ones that I produce and I cannot make him stop."

So the boys began to make arrows, and they gathered dry pine sticks and began to heat rocks, and the long Otter came towards them.

As it opened its mouth the boys shot arrows into it; and as that did not stop it from drawing nearer, they threw the hot rocks down its throat, and it curled up and died afterwards. They were taken up and carried through the air and gently placed upon the ground near their homes, where they lived for many years.

OLD MAN AT THE BEGINNING

(Crow)

At the beginning of the world, there was nothing but water. It was dark in the world, and no one saw the water of the world.

Then the Old Man of the Crow People came into the world, and he looked all around and said, "Is there nothing in this world but water?"

Off in the distance, Old Man saw that there were two little ducks swimming about. These ducks had red eyes. Old Man called them to him. They came swimming, paddling in the world of water.

Old Man said to them, "Is there nothing in this world but water?"

The Elder Duck answered, "We have never seen anything in this world but water, but we think that there may be something down under the water. We feel it in our hearts."

"Dive down, Younger Duck," said Old Man, and the Younger Duck dove deep under the water, looking for the bottom. He was gone a long time, and Old Man said, "Oh, I am afraid Younger Duck has drowned."

"No," said the Elder Duck, "we are able to hold our breath for a long time. He will come back up." At about that time, Younger Duck came up with something in his bill. It was a root.

"If there is a root," said Old Man, "then there must be earth as well. Dive down Elder Duck, and see if you find some earth."

The Elder Duck dove deep, and was gone for a very long time. When he came up, he had a ball of mud in his bill.

"This is what I have been looking for," said Old Man. He took the root and put it in the ball of wet earth, and blew three times on it. Once he blew, twice he blew, and again he blew on the ball of earth. The ball began to grow and fill the world and push the water aside. It grew until there was a great land, with many plants and animals living on it.

The Ducks, which live in water, on land, and in the sky, brought up the earth, and Old Man made the world for the Crow People.

FIRST JOURNEY THROUGH GRAND CANYON

(Hopi)

Long ago, on the edge of the Grand Canyon in Arizona, lived the ancestors of the Snake Clan, who belonged to the Hopi Indian tribe.

Chief of the Hopis had a very wise son, who liked to sit and meditate on the edge of the canyon. He tried many times to imagine where the powerful river far below finally ended.

Experienced Old Men of their nation did not know the answer for Wise Son. Their council leaders had different ideas among themselves. One thought the river took a secret course through huge underground passages. Another thought it entered the middle of the world and there it cared for large and dangerous reptiles.

Eagerly, Wise Son said to his father, the Chief, "Is it not time for me to seek my answer? I wish to go down the great river and find the place where it ends."

Proud of his son's desire for his answer, the Chief gladly granted him permission to go. Wise Son, overjoyed with his coming venture, planned specifically for every need. His family and tribal friends helped him to design and to build a waterproof boat that could be closed entirely, like a cocoon.

He constructed a long pushing pole to help him navigate the waters. The Shaman tied prayer sticks at the top of the pole, with special blessings for a safe journey.

Finally, the day arrived for Wise Son to leave in his special canoe. The Chief and his warriors arrived with supplies of food, good wishes, and more prayer sticks.

Week after week, Wise Son drifted with the river. He was happy. He learned to keep his canoe in the main current, though it carried him through several turbulent side routes, including rapids and tunnel like caves. He successfully came though these experiences with joy in his heart.

On and on, Wise Son travelled. He found his way out of steep canyons and through flat meadowlands. He caught fresh fish for his food. One day, Wise Son noticed a change in the taste of the water. It was salty and he knew that he should not drink it. Then to his surprise, he suddenly floated into a great body of water that extended as far as he could see. He had discovered the place where the mighty river ended, in the ocean where the sun sleeps!

He saw an island and guided his boat to its shore. There was a house nearby. He found only a very small entrance door. He knocked and asked, "Please, will you let me come in and see you?"

Spider Woman, who possessed spiritual power, lived there and answered, "Please make the hole large enough and enter."

This, Wise Son did and sat down inside. He presented to Spider Woman one of his prayer sticks and told her of his adventure to find the place where the river ended.

"When I return to my tribe, I wish to take with me a gift that might be helpful to my people," he said.

"There is a neighboring house where there are many beautiful ornaments like beads and rocks. These might be gifts that you can take to your people," she replied. "But I must warn you to be careful of the fierce animals on the path. I will give you some of my magic lotion to protect you."

Together they started for the treasure house. To guide him, Spider Woman sat upon Wise Son's ear, where she could whisper to him.

Immediately, Wise Son sprinkled some magic lotion on the marshy path. A colorful bridge appeared instantly, guiding them across the marsh to the treasure house.

First, they encountered an enormous lion like animal showing its fangs. Wise Son tossed him a prayer stick and sprinkled magic lotion, which calmed the creature.

Second, they met a bear like animal; third, a mad cat like creature; fourth, a ferocious wolf like beast; fifth, a huge angry looking snake with rattles on its tail. Wise Son quieted all of them with Spider Woman's magic lotion.

The treasure house had steps leading to the roof, and from there steps took them down into a large room. Men squatted around the inside walls. The warriors wore handsome, bright colored beads hanging about their necks. They had painted their faces.

Wise Son squatted by the fire. All remained quiet for some time. The men gazed at Wise Son constantly. Finally, their Chief arose and lighted his pipe. After smoking four times, he passed the pipe to the stranger. Wise Son smoked the magic number of times that seemed to please the Chief and the others. They then greeted him in a friendly manner, as if he were one of their own.

In return for their warm welcome, Wise Son gave to each man a prayer stick tipped with special feathers made by ancient Hopi warriors.

"Now it is time to put on our snake costumes," announced the Chief.

Wise Son observed that skins of enormous snakes were suspended from the ceiling, around all four walls. He was asked to face about, so that he would not see how the warriors got into their snakeskin costumes.

When Wise Son was asked to turn back, he saw snakes of many sizes and colors, hissing and writhing over the dirt floor. Spider Woman remained on Wise Son's ear.

"Be strong," she whispered to him. "The snakes will not hurt you, only frighten you. Do whatever I tell you."

The Chief of the Snake People had made his daughter become a yellow snake with rattles. Wise Son did not know this, and he was asked to choose the Chief's daughter. If he could choose correctly, the Snake People would show him their ceremonial dance. They also would give him many beads and stones to take to his nation.

Wise Son tried very hard to guess which snake was the Chief's daughter. Spider Woman whispered in his ear, "Choose the yellow one with rattles."

Wise Son did, and yellow snake with rattles suddenly became the loveliest and fairest of Indian maidens. He knew immediately that he could easily fall in love with her.

That evening the Chief and his warriors gave to Wise Son all the secrets of the Snake Ceremony. They taught him the words of praise and thanksgiving, which they sang for him. They showed him the ceremonial steps, which they danced for him. They showed him how they put on their snake costumes. Finally, they showed him their religious altar.

After Wise Son learned all that he should know, he and Spider Woman crossed the bridge and returned to her house. He presented her with another prayer stick, as he thanked her for her help. In return, she gave him a beautiful bead of turquoise from her north room. She gave him a white shell from her east room. From her south room, she gave him a red bead, and from her west room a larger turquoise. She then gave him a bag of special beads for his nation, but she warned him not to open it on the way home.

Next morning, Wise Son went back to the house of the Snake People to say farewell. Their Chief welcomed him and declared, "You have gained our friendship and my beautiful daughter. Take her for your wife. We wish you happiness and a pleasant journey back to your nation."

The tribe gave them many presents of good clothing and much food to send the happy couple on their way home.

They took the overland route following the great river. Each day Wise Son found the treasure bag heavier and heavier. He and his wife could hardly carry it between them. One day out of extreme curiosity, they opened the bag and looked inside.

Regardless of Spider Woman's caution, the two rolled out the beads and made strands for each to wear around their necks. By the following morning, all of the gift beads had vanished. Only remaining were the stones from the four rooms in Spider Woman's house.

Many moons later, the young couple reached home on the far edge of the Grand Canyon. Wise Son was delighted to be home again after his great adventure. The entire Hopi nation rejoiced over his safe return and welcomed his new young wife to their nation.

Wise Son told where the great river ended. He told them about the Snake Clan, and that he and his wife brought them a special ceremony from the Snake People, living where the sun sleeps.

Wise Son and his wife taught the Hopis all the songs and dances of the Snake Ceremony. This was the beginning of the Snake Clan of the Hopi nation.

THE ROOSTER, THE MOCKINGBIRD AND THE MAIDEN

(Hopi)

In the old days many Hopis lived at Oraibi, with birds and animals living as equals among them. At the northwest pueblo lived a beautiful maiden who persistently refused all offers of marriage. The young men of Oraibi brought gifts to her, hoping to win her as a wife, but she returned their presents and sent them away.

Far away to the North a powerful Chief heard of her beauty and made the long journey to Oraibi to win her consent to marry. He brought with him a bundle of presents, which he set down outside her house before entering to introduce himself. He found the girl grinding cornmeal.

Without stopping her work, she looked up at the handsome visitor, but said nothing.

"Why do you not talk to me?" he asked.

"Who are you, going around here?" she replied.

"I came to ask you to marry me," he said. "I left my gifts outside. Go and look at them."

The girl stopped her grinding, went outside, and found a large basket woven of bright yellow reeds. She brought it into the house, and opening it found two yellow bridal robes, a pair of yellow moccasins, and a wide yellow belt. After looking at the gifts for a moment, she put them back into the basket and handed it to the young Chief "I do not want them," she said. "I do not want you. You may go now."

The young man bowed his head, picked up the basket, and left.

Now, over on another side of Oraibi lived a Rooster, a very proud Rooster, who could assume the appearance of a man whenever he chose to do so. That afternoon he heard about the visit of the Chief from the North, and he thought it strange that this beautiful maiden had sent the powerful Chief away. So curious was he that he made preparations to visit her that very evening. Changing himself into a handsome young man, the Rooster dressed in a red shirt figured with black lines. He also wore turquoise ear pendants, and on top of his head a bunch of red feathers. When he went up into the girl's house he found her drying cornmeal in a pot over a fire, and he could tell at once that she was pleased by his appearance.

The Rooster acted like a perfect gentleman, seating himself by the side of the fireplace and complimenting her on the fine art objects she had assembled in the room. Pleased by his remarks, the girl began chatting merrily with him. When he arose and boldly asked her to marry him, the girl told him to return in four days and she would do so.

Being a very proud Rooster, he was not surprised that the girl had accepted him instead of sending him away as she had all her other suitors. "Very well," he said, "I shall return in four days."

Now, there was a Mockingbird who lived in a peach orchard somewhat south of that pueblo. On the third day after the Rooster visited the beautiful girl, the Mockingbird heard about it. This Mockingbird was a strong rival of the Rooster, and he was extremely angry to learn that the girl had agreed to marry him. Like the Rooster, the Mockingbird possessed the power to change himself into a man. He did so immediately, dressed himself splendidly, and hurried over to visit the maiden. He had made himself so handsome, and his voice was so musical that the girl was quite bewitched by him. She went to tell her mother that she had changed her mind. She would marry the Mockingbird instead of the Rooster.

"Very well," her mother said, "if you think you can trust him."

Meanwhile the Rooster, who had grown so in love with of the girl that he spent most of his time watching her house in hopes of catching sight of her, happened to see the Mockingbird go up to the pueblo. After a while the Rooster's curiosity turned to jealousy and he ran up to the door of the girl's house and knocked. Without waiting to be admitted, he entered and found the Mockingbird sitting by the fireplace. "What are you doing here?" he shouted at the Mockingbird.

"I have come to marry this maiden," the Mockingbird replied.

"Not so," the Rooster said. "Tomorrow it is I who shall marry her. You are not worthy of her. I own all these people here in Oraibi. They are mine. When I crow in the morning they all get up.

"I am worth more than you," retorted the Mockingbird. "When I twitter and sing in the morning I make the sun come up."

"Very well," the Rooster said. "Let us compete with each other and see who is worth the most. In three days we shall have a contest and see who can make the sun rise. Until then no one shall marry the maiden."

The Mockingbird agreed and they both left the girl's house. When the Rooster returned home he sat down and thought of how he could beat the Mockingbird by making the sun rise. He knew there was no use asking for help from the God of the Eagle Clan, the Great Thunderbird, because he favored Mockingbirds. Finally the Rooster decided to go to Moenkopi and ask the wisest of the Roosters and Hens who lived there to teach him how to make the sun rise.

It was a long distance to Moenkopi, and by the time the Rooster reached Bow Mound he was so weary that he feared he could go no farther. He sat down on a stone beside a shrine to rest, and when he did so an opening appeared in the shrine and he heard a voice say, "Come in."

He entered and was greeted by several beautiful girls, one of whom brought him a tray of shelled corn. He picked and ate it like Roosters eat.

When he was no longer hungry, the girl said, "You were tired from running so far. Now you have the strength to reach your destination."

The Rooster thanked the girls and went out. Feeling somewhat energized, he continued his journey, running very fast until he reached Moenkopi.

There he came to a steep bluff which he descended by a ladder to a large rock with an opening closed by a heavy door. The Rooster crowed repeatedly until the door was opened and a voice invited him to enter. Inside he found many Roosters and Hens of all ages. They seemed pleased that he had come to see them, offered him a place to sit, and brought him some shelled corn.

"What brings you to honor us with your presence?" the Chief Rooster asked politely.

"At Oraibi a Mockingbird and I are contending over a maiden," the Rooster replied. "We are contesting to see which of us has the most power. When I crow in the morning all the people get up, but when the Mockingbird sings the sun comes up. I want you to teach me how to make the sun rise and bring light to the world."

"Very well," the Rooster Chief said. "We shall at least try. The Mockingbird is very powerful and he has the help of the Great Thunderbird, but we shall at least try."

When evening came the Roosters and Hens gathered and sang into the night. After they finished singing four long songs the Roosters all crowed. Then they sang four more songs, and crowed again. After singing three more songs they crowed a third time. By now the yellow dawn was appearing, and after they sang two more songs, the sun rose above the edge of the earth.

"We have done what needed to be done," the Chief Rooster said. "Now you can go home and show the Mockingbird that you can make the sun come up."

The Rooster started back to Oraibi, running very fast. Again, when he reached Bow Mound he fell exhausted by the shrine and went inside. "I am too worn out to run any farther," he said to the girls. "I shall never get home in time."

They laughed at him and brought him some shelled corn. "Of course you will get home in time," they assured him. "We shall dress you up and then you will get home in time." While he was eating they stood behind him so he could not see them fastening dry corn husks to his tail feathers.

When he started running toward Oraibi, the corn husks rattled loudly. He was so frightened by the rattling that he ran very fast, never looking back, all the way to his house. When he went inside, he found the corn husks on his tail and removed them.

He rested all night and the next morning he felt very strong. Late in the day he walked pass the pueblo to the peach orchard where the Mockingbird lived and told him to come over to his house that night for the contest. After the Rooster left, the Mockingbird went to see the Great Thunderbird and informed him that the time had come to prove his power over the sun.

That evening the Mockingbird came to the Rooster's house to wait for the next dawn. That night the Rooster sang and crowed until the first yellow of daylight appeared. Then he finished the last two songs he had learned at Moenkopi and began crowing with all his might.

About this time, however, the Great Thunderbird flew up and spread his large wings across the eastern sky, completely covering up the dawn. No matter how loud the Rooster crowed, the sun did not hear him and would not rise.

The Mockingbird laughed at the Rooster. "You have failed," he said. "Now it is my turn. Come to my house tonight and I will show you how it is done."

That evening the Rooster went to the Mockingbird's house. After darkness fell the Mockingbird sang four long songs and then whistled. He waited a while and sang three more songs and whistled, and the dawn began to appear. He then sang his last two songs, and very slowly the sun rose above the edge of the earth. "You see," the Mockingbird cried triumphantly, "only I can make the sun come up."

"Yes," the Rooster admitted, "you have great powers. You know how to make the sun rise. You have won the maiden for your wife."

And so the Mockingbird married the beautiful girl. Later on, the Rooster also found himself a wife, one not nearly so beautiful. By and by children were born. Those of the Mockingbird talked and jabbered constantly like their father, but the children of the Rooster were kind and gentle and did not talk so much.

HOW THE BEETLES PRODUCED PAIN

(Hopi)

In the Oraibi village lived the Black Beetles. It was always hot and the wind was blowing, and it did not rain. As these Beetles drink rain water they became very thirsty. Some became so thirsty that they died.

So their Chief said one time, "Let us have a dance and perhaps if we dance it will rain, because if it does not rain we shall all die!"

"Very well, we shall have a dance," the Beatles said, "and maybe it will rain then, and we shall not die."

So one evening they assembled to practice for the dance and their Chief made a little song for them. This they were practicing. They practiced a while in the evening, and then they went to sleep.

The next day they were going to have their dance. Early in the morning they got up and their Chief made four prayer feathers for them. He deposited the prayer feathers west of their village, and spoke to the clouds in the San Francisco mountains saying, "We are thirsty here, so you come quickly this way and bring us some water that we may drink and not die."

So he returned to their village and they dressed up for the dance. They painted their bodies black, and then they danced. They were in a hurry because they were thirsty.

Their Chief began to pray to the clouds in the San Francisco Mountains. "Come this way quickly and bring us water."

So they were formed in a line now and one of them acted as leader. By this time a cloud was forming in the mountains. They now sang the following song,

Yoookwaa yoookwahayaha,

Rain, rain.

Ihi, aha, ihi.

As they were singing, the clouds came nearer and it began to rain and thunder, and the water began to fall so that they could now drink. When they had quenched their thirst they were very happy and ran about because they were no longer thirsty.

HOW A PIEGAN WARRIOR FOUND THE FIRST HORSES

(Blackfoot)

A long time ago a warrior of the Piegan Blackfoot dreamed about a lake far away where some large animals lived. A voice in the dream told him the animals were harmless, and that he could use them for dragging travois and carrying packs in the same way the Indians used dogs. "Go to this lake," the dream voice told him, "and take a rope with you so that you can catch these animals."

When the Piegan awoke he took a long rope made from strips of buffalo hide and travelled many miles on foot to the shore of the lake. He dug a hole in the sandy beach and hide himself there. While he watched, he saw many animals come down to the lake to drink. Deer, Coyotes, Elk and Buffalo all came to quench their thirsts.

After a while the wind began to blow. Waves rose upon the lake and began to roll and hiss along the beach. At last a herd of large animals, unlike any the Piegan had ever seen before, suddenly appeared before him. They were as large as Elks, and had small ears and long tails hanging to the ground. Some were white, and some black, and some red and spotted. The young ones were smaller. When they reached the water's edge and bent their heads to drink, the voice of the man he heard in his dream whispered to him, "Throw your rope and catch one."

And so the Piegan threw his rope and caught one of the largest of the animals. It struggled, pulled, and dragged the man about, but he was not strong enough to hold the animal. Finally it pulled the rope out of his hands, and the whole herd ran into the lake and sank out of sight beneath the water.

Feeling very sad, the Piegan returned to camp. He went into his lodge and prayed for help to the voice he had heard in his dream.

The voice answered him, “Four times you may try to catch these animals. If in four times trying you do not catch them, you will never see them again.”

Before he went to sleep that night the Piegan asked Old Man to help him, and while he slept Old Man told him that he was not strong enough to catch one of the big animals.

“Try to catch one of the young animals,” Old Man said, “and then you can hold it.”

Next morning the Piegan went again to the shores of the big lake, and again he dug a hole in the sand and lay hidden there while the Deer, the Coyotes, the Elk and the Buffalo came to drink. At last the wind began to rise and the waves rolled and hissed upon the beach. Then came the herd of strange animals to drink at the lake, and again the man threw his rope. This time he caught one of the young animals and was able to hold it.

One by one he caught all the young animals out of the herd and led them back to the Piegan camp. After they had been there a little while, the mares, the mothers of these colts, came trotting into the camp. Their udders were filled with milk for the colts to drink. Soon after the mares came, the stallions of the herd followed them into the camp.

At first the Piegans were afraid of these new animals and would not go near them, but the warrior who had caught them told everybody that they would not harm them. After a while the animals became so tame that they followed the people whenever they moved their camp from place to place. Then the Piegans began to put packs on them, and they called this animal po-no-kah- mita, or Elk Dog, because they were big and shaped like an Elk and could carry a pack like a dog.

That is how the Piegan Blackfoot got their horses.

THE GHOSTS' BUFFALO

(Blackfoot)

A long time ago there were four Blackfeet, who went to war against the Crees. They traveled a long way, and at last their horses gave out, and they started back toward their homes. As they were going along they came to the Sand Hills; and while they were passing through them, they saw in the sand a fresh travois trail, where people had been travelling.

One of the men said, "Let us follow this trail until we come up with some of our people. Then we will camp with them."

They followed the trail for a long way and after awhile one powerful Blackfeet, said to the others, "Why follow this longer? It is just nothing."

The others said, "Not so. These are our people. We will go on and camp with them."

They went on, and toward evening, one of them found a stone maul and a dog travois.

He said, "Look at these things. I know this maul and this travois. They belonged to my mother, who died. They were buried with her. This is strange." He took the things. When night came the men camped.

Early in the morning, they heard, all about them, sounds as if a camp of people were there. They heard a young man shouting a sort of war cry, as young men do; women chopping wood; a man calling for a feast, asking people to come to his lodge and smoke, all the different sounds of the camp. They looked about, but could see nothing; and then they were frightened and covered their heads with their robes. At last they took courage, and started to look around and see what they could learn about this strange thing.

For a little while they saw nothing, but pretty soon one of them said, "Look over there. See that pis'kun. Let us go over and look at it." As they were going toward it, one of them picked up a stone pointed arrow.

He said, "Look at this. It belonged to my father. This is his place." They started to go on toward the pis'kun, but suddenly they could see no pis'kun. It had disappeared all at once.

A little while after this, one of them spoke up, and said, "Look over there. There is my father Running Buffalo. There! He has killed. Let us go over to him."

They all looked where this man pointed, and they could see a person on a white horse, running buffalo. While they were looking, the person killed the buffalo, and got off his horse to butcher it. They started to go over toward him, and saw him at work butchering, and saw him turn the buffalo over on its back; but before they got to the place where he was, the person got on his horse and rode off, and when they got to where he had been skinning the buffalo, they saw lying on the ground only a dead mouse. There was no buffalo there. By the side of the mouse was a buffalo chip, and lying on it was an arrow painted red.

The man said, "That is my father's arrow. That is the way he painted them." He took it up in his hands; and when he held it in his hands, he saw that it was not an arrow but a blade of spear grass. Then he laid it down, and it was an arrow again.

Another Blackfoot found a buffalo rock.

Sometime after this, the men got home to their camp. The man who had taken the maul and the dog travois, when he got home and smelled the smoke from the fire, died, and so did his horse. It seems that the shadow of the person who owned the things was angry at him and followed him home. Two others of these Blackfeet have since died, killed in war; but one is alive yet.

He is the one who took a stone and an iron arrow point that had belonged to his father, and always carried them about with him. That is why he has lived so long. The man who took the stone arrow point found near the pis'kun, which had belonged to his father, took it home with him. This was his medicine. After that he was badly wounded in two fights, but he was not killed; he got well.

THE STORY OF THE BUFFALO DANCE

(Blackfoot)

When the Buffalo first came to be upon the land, they were not friendly to the Indian. When the hunters tried to coax them over the cliffs for the good of the villages, they were unwilling to offer themselves up.

They did not enjoy being turned into blankets and dried flesh for winter rations. They did not want their hooves and horn to become tools and utensils nor did they welcome their ligaments being used for sewing.

"No, No," they said. "We won't fall into your traps. And we will not fall for your tricks."

So when the hunters guided them towards the cliffs, they would always turn aside at the very last moment. With this lack of cooperation, it seemed the Indians would be hungry and cold and ragged all winter long.

One of the hunters had a daughter who was very proud of her father's skill with the bow. During the fullness of summer, he always brought her the best of hides to dress, and she in turn would work the deerskins into the softest, whitest of clothes for him to wear. Her own dresses were like the down of a snow goose, and the moccasins she made for the children and the grandmothers in the village were the most welcome of gifts.

But now with the hint of snow in the wind, and Deer becoming scarcer in the willow breaks, she could see this unwillingness on the part of the Buffalo families could become a real problem.

Hunter's Daughter decided she would do something about it.

She went to the base of the cliff and looked up. She began to sing in a low, soft voice, "Oh, Buffalo Family, come down and visit me. If you come down and feed my relatives in a wedding feast, I will join your family as the bride of your strongest warrior."

As she stopped and listened, she thought she heard the slight rumbling sound of thunder in the distance.

Again she sang, "Oh, Buffalo Family, come down and visit me. Feed my family in a wedding feast so that I may be a bride."

The thunder was much louder now. Suddenly the Buffalo Family began falling from the sky at her feet. One very large Buffalo Bull landed on top of the others, and walked across the backs of his relatives to stand before hunter's daughter.

"I am here to claim you as my bride," said Large Buffalo.

"Oh, but now I am afraid to go with you," said Hunter's Daughter.

"Ah, but you must," said Large Buffalo, "For my people have come to provide your people with a wedding feast. As you can see, they have offered themselves up."

"Yes, but I must run and tell my relatives the good news," said Hunter's Daughter.

"No," said Large Buffalo. No word need be sent. You are not getting away so easily."

And with that said, Large Buffalo lifted her between his horns and carried her off to his village in the rolling grass hills.

The next morning the whole village was out looking for Hunter's Daughter. When they found the mound of Buffalo below the cliff, the father, who was in fact a fine tracker as well as a skilled hunter, looked at his daughter's footprints in the dust.

"She's gone off with a Buffalo, he said. I shall follow them and bring her back."

So he walked out upon the plains, with only his bow and arrows. He walked and walked a great distance until he was so tired that he had to sit down to rest beside a buffalo wallow.

Along came Magpie and sat down beside him.

Hunter spoke to Magpie in a respectful tone, “Oh knowledgeable bird, has my daughter been stolen from me by a Buffalo? Have you seen them? Can you tell me where they have gone?”

Magpie replied with understanding, “Yes, I have seen them pass this way. They are resting just over this hill.”

“Well,” said Hunter, would you kindly take my daughter a message for me? Will you tell her I am here just over the hill?”

So Magpie flew to where Large Buffalo lay asleep with his relatives in the dry prairie grass. He hopped over to where Hunter’s Daughter was quilling moccasins, as she sat dutifully beside her sleeping husband. “Your father is waiting for you on the other side of the hill,” whispered Magpie to the maiden.

“Oh, this is very dangerous,” she told him. These Buffalo are not friendly to us and they might try to hurt my father if he should come this way. Please tell him to wait for me and I will try to slip away to see him.”

Just then her husband, Large Buffalo, awoke and took off his horn. “Go bring me a drink from the wallow just over this hill,” said her husband.

So she took the horn in her hand and walked very casually over the hill.

Her father motioned silently for her to come with him, as he bent into a low crouch in the grass.

“No,” she whispered. The Buffalo are angry with our people who have killed their people. They will run after us and trample us into the dirt. I will go back and see what I can do to calm their feelings.”

And so Hunter’s daughter took the horn of water back to her husband who gave a loud snort when he took a drink. The snort turned into a bellow and all of the Buffalo got up in alarm. They all put their tails in the air and danced a Buffalo Dance over the hill, trampling the Hunter to pieces.

His daughter sat down on the edge of the wallow and broke into tears.

"Why are you crying?" said her Buffalo husband.

"You have killed my father and I am a prisoner, besides," she sobbed.

"Well, what of my people?" her husband replied. We have given our children, our parents and some of our wives up to your relatives in exchange for your presence among us. A deal is a deal."

But after thinking about her feelings, Large Buffalo knelt down beside her and said to her, "If you can bring your father back to life again, we will let him take you back home to your people."

So Hunter's Daughter started to sing a little song. "Magpie, Magpie help me find some piece of my father which I can mend back whole again."

Magpie appeared and sat down in front of her with his head cocked to the side.

"Magpie, Magpie, please see what you can find," she sang softly to the wind which bent the grasses slightly apart. Magpie cocked his head to the side and looked carefully within the layered folds of the grasses as the wind sighed again.

Quickly he picked out a piece of her father that had been hidden there, a little bit of bone.

"That will be enough to do the trick," said Hunter's Daughter, as she put the bone on the ground and covered it with her blanket.

Then she started to sing a refreshing song that had the power to bring injured people back to the land of the living. Quietly she sang the song that her grandmother had taught her. After a few passages, there was a lump under the blanket.

She and Magpie looked under the blanket and could see a man, but the man was not breathing. He lay cold as stone. So Hunter's Daughter continued to sing, softer and softer, so as not to startle her father as he began to move. When he stood up, alive and strong, the Buffalo People were amazed.

The Buffalo People said to Hunter's Daughter, "Will you sing this song for us after every hunt? We will teach your people the Buffalo Dance, so that whenever you dance before the hunt, you will be assured a good result. Then you will sing this song for us, and we will all come back to live again."

BATTLE WITH THE SNAKES

(Iroquois)

There was a man, called Djisdaah, who was not kind to animals. One day when Djisdaah was hunting, he found a Rattlesnake and decided to torture it. He held its head to the ground and pierced it with a piece of bark. Then as it was caught there, Djisdaah tormented it.

"We shall fight," Djisdaah said and then burned the Snake until it was dead. He thought this was a great joke and so, whenever he found a Snake, he would do the same thing.

One day another man from his village was walking through the forest when he heard a strange sound. It was louder than the wind hissing through the tops of tall pine trees. He crept closer to see. There, in a great clearing, were many Snakes. They had gathered for a war council and as he listened in fright.

"We shall now fight with them. Djisdaah has challenged us and we shall go to war. In four days we shall go to their village and fight them."

The man crept away and then ran as fast as he could to his village to tell what he had heard and seen. The Chief sent other warriors to see if the report was true. They returned in great fear.

"Ahhhh," they said, "it is so. The Snakes are all gathering to have a war."

The Chief of the village could see that he had no choice. "We must fight," he said and ordered the people of the village to make arrangements for the battle. They cut mountains of wood and stacked it in long piles all around the village. They built rows of stakes close together to keep the snakes out. When the fourth day came, the Chief ordered the wood be set on fire. Just as he did so they heard a great noise, like a great wind in the trees. It was the noise of the Snakes, hissing as they came to the village to do battle.

Usually a Snake will not go near a fire, but these Snakes were determined to have their revenge. They went straight into the flames. Many of them died, but the living Snakes crawled over the bodies of the dead ones and continued to move forward until they reached the second row of stakes.

Once again, the Chief ordered that the piles of wood in the second row of defense be set on fire. But the Snakes crawled straight into the flames, hissing their war songs, and the living crawled over the bodies of the dead. It was a terrible sight. They reached the second row of stakes and, even though the people fought bravely, it was no use. There were so many Snakes they could not be stopped. Soon they forced their way past the last row of stakes and the people of the village were fighting for their lives. The first man to be killed was Djisdaah, the one who had challenged the Snakes to battle.

It was now clear that they could never win this battle. The Chief shouted to the Snakes who had reached the edge of the village, "Hear me, my brothers. We surrender to you. We have done you a great wrong. Have mercy on us."

The Snakes stopped where they were and there was a great silence. The exhausted warriors looked at the great army of Snakes and the Snakes stared back at them. Then the earth trembled and cracked of them. A great Snake, a Snake taller than the biggest pine tree, whose head was larger than a great long house, lifted himself out of the crack in the earth.

"Hear me," he said. "I am the Chief of all the Snakes. We shall go and leave you in peace if you will agree to two things."

The Chief looked at the great Snake and nodded his head. "We will agree, Great Chief," he said.

"It is well," said the Chief of the Snakes. "These are the two things. First, you must always treat my people with respect. Secondly, as long as the world stands, you will never name another man Djisdaah."

And so it was agreed and so it is, even today.

THE TREE BOUND

(Dakota)

On a clear summer day a large yellow Sun hung directly overhead. The singing of Birds filled the summer space between earth and sky with sweet music. Again and again sang a yellow breasted Bird "Koda Ni Dakota!" He insisted upon it. "Koda Ni Dakota!" which was "Friend, you're a Dakota! Friend, you're a Dakota!"

Perhaps the Bird meant the righter of wrongs with the sacred arrow, for there across the plain he strode. He was handsome in his paint and feathers, proud with his great buckskin quiver on his back and a long bow in his hand. From an Eastern camp of cone shaped teepees he was going. Over the Indian village hovered a large Red Eagle threatening the safety of the people. Every morning rose this terrible Red Eagle out of a high chalk bluff and spreading out his huge wings soared slowly over the camp ground. Then it was that the people, terror stricken, ran screaming into their lodges. Covering their heads with their blankets, they sat trembling with fear. No one dared to go out till the Red Eagle had disappeared beyond the west, where meet the blue and green.

The Chief of the tribe tried to find among his warriors a powerful warrior who could send a death arrow to the Red Eagle. At last to urge his warriors to try he made his Medicine Man announce a new reward.

Of the Chieftain's two beautiful daughters he would have his choice who brought the dreaded Red Eagle with an arrow in its breast.

Upon hearing these words, the warriors of the village, both young and old, both heroes and cowards, trimmed new arrows for the reward. At first dawn there stood under the shadow of the high chalk bluff many warriors; silent as ghosts and wrapped in robes gathered tightly about their waists, they waited with their bow and arrow.

Some cunning old warriors stayed not with the group. They crouched low upon the open ground. But all eyes alike were fixed upon the top of the high chalk bluff. Breathless they watched for the soaring of the Red Eagle.

From within the teepees many eyes peeped through the small holes in the front lapels. With shaking knees and hard set teeth, the women looked out upon the Dakota warriors prowling about with bows and arrows.

At length when the morning Sun also peeped over the Eastern horizon at the armed Dakotas' warriors, the Red Eagle walked out upon the edge of the high chalk bluff. Pluming his beautiful feathers, he ruffled his neck and flapped his strong wings together. Then he dived into the air. Slowly he winged his way over the camp ground; over the warriors with their strong bows and arrows! In an instant the long bows were bent. Strong straight arrows with red feathered tips sped upward to the blue sky. Slowly the Red Eagle's wings moved, untouched by the poison tipped arrows. Off to the West beyond the reach of arrow, beyond the reach of eye, the Red Eagle flew away.

A sudden yell of high pitched voices broke the deadly silence of the dawn. The women talked excitedly about the untouched red of the Eagle's feathers, while the warriors sulked within their teepees.

"He-he-he!" yelled the Chief.

On the evening of the same day sat a group of warriors around a bright burning fire. They were talking of a strange young warrior whom they spied while out upon a hunt for Deer beyond the bluffs. They saw the stranger taking aim. Following the point of his arrow with their eyes, they saw a herd of Buffalo. The arrow sprang from the bow! It darted into the skull of the foremost Buffalo. But unlike other arrows it pierced through the head of the creature and spinning in the air lit into the next Buffalo head. One by one the Buffalo fell upon the sweet grass they were grazing. With straight trembling limbs they lay on their sides.

The young warrior stood calmly by, counting on his fingers the Buffalo as they dropped dead to the ground. When the last one fell, he ran picking up his sacred arrow wiped it carefully on the soft grass. He slipped it into his long fringed quiver.

"He is going to make a feast for some hungry tribe!" cried the warriors among themselves as they hastened away.

They were afraid of the warrior with the sacred arrow. When the warrior's tale of the warrior's sacred arrow reached the ears of the Chief, his face brightened with a smile. He sent forth warriors, to learn of him his birth, his name, and his deeds.

"If he is the righter of wrongs with the sacred arrow, sprung up from the earth out of a clot of Buffalo blood, bid him come to me. Let him kill the Red Eagle with his sacred arrow. Let him win for himself one of my beautiful daughters," he had said to his warriors.

After four days and nights the warriors returned. "He is coming," they said. "We have seen him. He is straight and tall; handsome in face, with large black eyes. He paints his round cheeks with bright red, and wears lines of red over his temples like our men of sacred rank. He carries on his back a long fringed quiver in which he keeps his sacred arrow. His bow is long and strong. He is coming now to kill the Red Eagle." All around the camp ground from mouth to ear passed those words of the returned warriors.

Now it chanced that immortal Iktomi overheard the people talking. At once he was filled with a new desire. "If only I had the sacred arrow, I would kill the Red Eagle and win the Chief's daughter for a wife," said he in his heart.

Back to his lonely teepee he ran. Beneath the tree in front of his teepee he sat upon the ground with chin between his drawn up knees. His eyes scanned the wide plain. He was watching for the righter of wrongs.

"He is coming!" said the warriors. All of a sudden Iktomi raised an open palm to his brow and peered afar into the West. The summer Sun hung bright in the middle of a cloudless sky. There across the green prairie was a warrior walking bareheaded toward the East.

"Ha! Ha! Tis he! The warrior with the sacred arrow!" laughed Iktomi. When the Bird with the yellow breast sang loud again, "Koda Ni Dakota! Friend, you're a Dakota!" Iktomi put his hand over his mouth as he threw his head far backward, laughing at both the Bird and warrior.

"He is your friend, but his arrow will kill one of your kind! He is a Dakota, but soon he'll grow into the bark on this tree! Ha! Ha! Ha!" he laughed again.

The young righter of wrongs walked with long strides nearer and nearer toward the lonely teepee and tree. Iktomi heard the swish of the warrior's feet through the tall grass.

He was passing now beyond the tree, when Iktomi, springing to his feet, called out, "How, how, my friend! I see you are dressed in handsome deerskins and have red paint on your cheeks. You are going to some feast or dance, may I ask?" The young warrior only smiled and Iktomi went on, "I have not had a mouthful of food this day. Have pity on me, young warrior, and shoot yonder Bird for me!" With these words Iktomi pointed toward the tree top, where sat a Bird on the highest branch. The young righter of wrongs, always ready to help those in need, sent an arrow upward and the Bird fell. In the next branch it was caught between the forked prongs.

"My friend, climb the tree and get the Bird. I cannot climb so high. I would get dizzy and fall," pleaded Iktomi.

The righter of wrongs began to scale the tree, when Iktomi cried to him, "My friend, your beaded buckskins may be torn by the branches. Leave them safe upon the grass till you are down again."

"You are right," replied the young warrior, quickly slipping off his long fringed quiver. Together with his dangling pouches and tinkling ornaments, he placed it on the ground. Now he climbed the tree unrestricted. Soon from the top he took the Bird.

"My friend, toss to me your arrow that I may have the honor of wiping it clean on soft deerskin!" exclaimed Iktomi.

"How!" said the brave, and threw the Bird and arrow to the ground.

At once Iktomi seized the arrow. Rubbing it first on the grass and then on a piece of deerskin, he muttered unclear words all the while.

The young warrior, stepping downward from limb to limb, hearing the low muttering, said, "Iktomi, I cannot hear what you say!"

"Oh, my friend, I was only talking of your big heart," said Iktomi.

Again stooping over the arrow, Iktomi continued his repetition of charm words. "Grow fast, grow fast to the bark of the tree," he whispered.

Still the young warrior moved slowly downward. Suddenly dropping the arrow and standing erect, Iktomi said aloud: "Grow fast to the bark of the tree!" Before the warrior could leap from the tree, he became grown to the bark.

"Ah! Ha!" laughed the immortal Iktomi. "I have the sacred arrow! I have the beaded buckskins of the great retaliator!" Shouting and dancing beneath the tree, he said, "I shall kill the Red Eagle; I shall wed the Chief's beautiful daughter!"

"Oh, Iktomi, set me free!" begged the tree bound young warrior. But Iktomi's ears were like the fungus on a tree. He did not hear with them.

Wearing the handsome buckskins and carrying proudly the sacred arrow in his right hand, he started off Eastward. Imitating the swaying strides of the righter of wrongs, he walked away with a face turned slightly skyward.

"Oh, set me free! I am glued to the tree like its own bark! Cut me loose!" moaned the young warrior.

A young woman, carrying on her strong back a bundle of tightly bound willow sticks, passed near by the lonely teepee. She heard the wailing warrior's voice. She paused to listen to the sad words. Looking around she saw nowhere a human creature. "It may be a spirit," she thought.

"Oh! Cut me loose! Set me free! Iktomi has played me false! He has made me bark of his tree!" cried the voice again.

The young woman dropped her pack of firewood to the ground. With her stone axe she hurried to the tree. There before her astonished eyes clung a young warrior close to the tree.

Too shy for words, yet too kind hearted to leave the stranger tree bound, she cut loose the whole bark. Like a man, she drew it to the ground. With it came the young warrior also. Free once more, he started away. Looking backward, a few paces from the young woman, he waved his hand, upward and downward, before her face. This was a sign of gratefulness used when words failed to interpret strong emotion.

When the bewildered woman reached her dwelling, she mounted a pony and rode swiftly across the rolling land. To the camp ground in the East, to the Chief troubled by the Red Eagle, she carried her story.

THE WARLIKE SEVEN

(Dakota)

Once seven people went out to make war, they were the Ashes, the Fire, the Bladder, the Grasshopper, the Dragon Fly, the Fish, and the Turtle. As they were talking excitedly, waving their fists in violent gestures, a wind came and blew the Ashes away.

"Ho!" cried the others, "he cannot fight this one!"

The six went on running to make war more quickly. They descended a deep valley, the Fire going foremost until they came to a river.

The Fire said "Hsss—tchu!" and was gone.

"Ho!" cried the others, "he cannot fight this one!"

Therefore the five went on the more quickly to make war. They came to a great wood.

While they were going through it, the Bladder was heard to sneer and to say, "He! You should rise above these, brothers." With these words he went upward among the tree tops; and the thorn apple pricked him. He fell through the branches and was nothing!

"Ho!" cried the others, "he cannot fight this one!"

Still the others would not turn back. The four went boldly on to make war. The Grasshopper with his cousin, the Dragon Fly, went foremost. They reached a marshy place, and the swamp was very deep. As they waded through the mud, the Grasshopper's legs stuck, and he pulled them off!

He crawled upon a log and wept, "You see me, brothers, I cannot go!"

The Dragon Fly went on, crying for his cousin. He would not be comforted, for he loved his cousin dearly. The more he grieved, the louder he cried, till his body shook with great violence. He blew his red swollen nose with a loud noise so that his head came off his slender neck, and he was fallen upon the grass.

"You see how it is," said the Fish, lashing his tail impatiently, "these people were not warriors!"

"Come!" he said, "let us go on to make war."

Thus the Fish and the Turtle came to a large camp ground.

"Ho!" exclaimed the people of this round village of teepees, "Who are these little ones? What do they seek?"

Neither of the them carried weapons, and their unimposing build misled the curious people.

The Fish was spokesman. With a peculiar omission of syllables, he said: "Shu... hi pi!"

"What? What? What?" clamored eager voices of men and women.

Again the Fish said: "Shu... hi pi!" Everywhere stood young and old with a palm to an ear. Still no one guessed what the Fish had mumbled!

From the bewildered crowd witty old Iktomi came forward.

"He, listen!" he shouted, rubbing his mischievous palms together, for where there was any trouble brewing, he was always in the midst of it.

"This little strange man says, 'Zuya unhipi!' We come to make war!"

"Uun!" replied the people, suddenly stricken glum. "Let us kill the silly pair! They can do nothing! They do not know the meaning of the phrase. Let us build a fire and boil them both!"

"If you put us on to boil," said the Fish, "there will be trouble."

"Ho ho!" laughed the village folk. "We shall see."

And so they made a fire.

"I have never been so angered!" said the Fish.

The Turtle in a whispered reply said, "We shall die!"

When a pair of strong hands lifted the Fish over the sputtering water, he put his mouth downward.

"Whssh!" he said. He blew the water all over the people, so that many were burned and could not see. Screaming with pain, they ran away.

"Oh, what shall we do with these dreadful ones?" the people said.

Others exclaimed, "Let us carry them to the lake of muddy water and drown them!"

Instantly they ran with them. They threw the Fish and the Turtle into the lake. Toward the center of the large lake the Turtle dived.

There he peeped up out of the water and, waving a hand at the crowd, sang out, "This is where I live!"

The Fish swam hither and thither with such energetic darts that his back fin made the water fly. "E han!" whooped the Fish, "this is where I live!"

"Oh, what have we done!" said the frightened people, "this will be our undoing."

Then a wise Chief said, "Iya, the Eater, shall come and swallow the lake!"

So one young brave went running to fetch Iya, the Eater; and Iya drank all day at the lake till his belly was like the earth.

Then the Fish and the Turtle dived into the mud; and Iya said, "They are not in me." Hearing this the people cried greatly.

Iktomi wading in the lake had also been swallowed like a Gnat in the water. Within the great Iya, Iktomi was looking skyward. So deep was the water in the Eater's stomach that the surface of the swallowed lake almost touched the sky.

"I will go that way," said Iktomi and he struck his knife upward in the Eater's stomach, causing the water to spill out drowning the people of the village.

Now when the great water fell into its own bed, the Fish and the Turtle came to the shore. They went home as great warriors.

HOW THE BUFFALO HUNT BEGAN

(Cheyenne)

The Buffalo formerly ate man. The Magpie and the Hawk were on the side of the people, for neither ate the other or the people. These two Birds flew to a council between animals and men. At the council, all determined that a race would be held, the winners to eat the losers.

The course was long, and around a mountain. The swiftest Buffalo called Neika, meaning swift head. She believed she would win and entered the race. On the other hand, the people were afraid because of the long distance. They were trying to get medicine to prevent fatigue.

All the Birds and animals painted themselves for the race, and since that time they have all been brightly colored. Even the Water Turtle put red paint around his eyes. The Magpie painted white on his head, shoulders, and tail. At last all were ready for the race, and stood in a row for the start.

They ran and ran, making some loud noises in place of singing to help themselves to run faster. All small Birds, Turtles, Rabbits, Coyotes, Wolves, Flies, Ants, Insects, and Snakes were soon left far behind. When they approached the mountain Neika, was ahead; then came the Magpie, Hawk, and the people; the rest were strung out along the way. The dust rose so quickly that nothing could be seen.

All around the mountain Neika, led the race, but the two Birds knew they could win, and merely kept up with Neika until they neared the finish line, which was back at the starting place. Then both Birds whooshed by Neika, and won the race for man. As they flew the course, they had seen fallen animals and Birds all over the place, who had run themselves to death, turning the ground and rocks red from the blood.

The Buffalo then told their young to hide from the people, who were going out to hunt them; and also told them to take some human flesh with them for the last time. The young Buffaloes did this, and stuck that meat in front of their chests, beneath their throat. Therefore, the people do not eat that part of the Buffalo, believing it is part human flesh.

From that day forward the Cheyenne's began to hunt Buffalo. Since all the friendly animals and Birds were on the people's side, they are not eaten by people, but they do wear and use their beautiful feathers for ornaments.

A LITTLE BRAVE AND THE MEDICINE WOMAN

(Sioux)

A village of Indians moved out of winter camp and pitched their tents in a circle on high land overlooking a lake. A little way down the slope was a grave. Choke cherries had grown up, hiding the grave from view. But as the ground had sunk somewhat, the grave was marked by a slight hollow.

One of the brave going out to hunt took a short cut through the choke cherry bushes. As he pushed them aside he saw the hollow grave, but thought it was a washout made by the rains. But as he went to step over it, to his great surprise he stumbled and fell. Upset by his accident, he drew back and tried again; but again he fell. When he came back to the village he told the old warriors what had happened to him. They remembered then that a long time before there had been buried there a Medicine Woman. Doubtless it was her medicine that made him stumble.

The story of the brave's adventure spread through the camp and made many curious to see the grave. Among others were six little boys who were, however, rather timid, for they were in great awe of the dead Medicine Woman. But they had a little playmate named Brave, a mischievous little scoundrel, whose hair was always uncombed and tossed about and who was never quiet for a moment.

"Let us ask Brave to go with us," they said; and they went in a group to see him.

"All right," said Brave, "I will go with you. But I have something to do first. You go on around the hill that way, and I will hasten around this way, and meet you a little later near the grave."

So the six little boys went on as told until they came to a place near the grave. There they halted.

"Where is Brave?" they asked.

Now Brave, full of mischief, had thought to play a joke on his little friends. As soon as they were well out of sight he had sped around the hill to the shore of the lake and sticking his hands in the mud had rubbed it over his face, plastered it in his hair, and soiled his hands until he looked like a newly risen corpse with the flesh rotting from his bones. He then went and lay down in the grave and awaited the boys.

When the six little boys came they were more timid than ever when they did not find Brave; but they were afraid to go back to the village without seeing the grave, for fear the old warriors would call them cowards.

So they slowly approached the grave and one of them timidly called out, "Please, Medicine Woman, we won't disturb your grave. We only want to see where you lie. Don't be angry."

At once a thin quavering voice, like an old woman's, called out, "Han, han, takoja, hechetuya, hechetuya! Yes, yes, that's right, that's right."

The boys were frightened out of their mind, believing the old Medicine Woman had come to life.

"Oh, Medicine Woman," they gasped, "don't hurt us; please don't, we'll go."

Just then Brave raised his muddy face and hands up through the choke cherry bushes. With the oozy mud dripping from his face he looked like some spirit just raised from the grave. The boys screamed and one fainted. The rest ran yelling up the hill to the village, where each broke at once for his mother's teepee.

As all the tents in a Sioux camping circle face the center, the boys as they came tearing into camp were in plain view from the teepees. Hearing the screaming, every woman in camp ran to her teepee door to see what had happened. Just then little Brave, as badly scared as the rest, came rushing in after them, his hair on end and covered with mud and crying out, forgetting his appearance yelled, "It's me, it's me!"

The women yelped and bolted in fright from the village. Brave dashed into his mother's teepee, scaring her out of her mind. Dropping pots and kettles, she tumbled out of the tent to run screaming with the rest. Nor would a single villager come near poor little Brave until he had gone down to the lake and washed himself.

THE STORY OF THE PET CRANE

(Sioux)

There was once upon a time a man, Kutesan, who did not care to live with his tribe in a crowded camp, but preferred a secluded spot in the deep forest, to live with his wife and family of five children. The oldest of the children, a boy, was twelve years of age, and being the son of a distinguished hunter, soon took to roaming through the forest in search of small game.

One day during his hunting, he discovered a Crane's nest, with only one young Crane sitting it. No doubt some Fox or Weasel had eaten the rest of the Crane's brothers and sisters.

The boy said to himself, "I will take this poor little Crane home and will raise him as a pet for our baby. If I leave him here some hungry Fox will be sure to eat the poor little fellow."

He carried the young Crane home and it grew to be nearly as tall as the boy's five year old sister.

Being brought with humans, it soon grew to understand all the family said. Although it could not speak it took part in all the games played by the children.

Kutesan was the father of the family and a great hunter. He always had a plentiful supply of Deer, Antelope, Buffalo, and Beaver meats on hand, but there came a change. The game moved to some other area, where no deadly shot like Kutesan would be around to wipe out their fast decreasing population. Kutesan started out early one morning in hopes of discovering some of the game which had disappeared as suddenly as though the earth had swallowed them. Kutesan traveled the whole day, all to no purpose. It was late in the evening when he staggered into camp. He was nearly dead with fatigue. Hastily swallowing a cup of cherry bark tea, the only food the family had. Kutesan at once went to sleep and was soon in the sweet land of dreams. The children soon joined their father and the poor woman sat thinking how they could save their children from hunger.

Suddenly out upon the night air rang the cry of a Crane. Instantly the pet Crane awoke, stepped outside and answered the call. The Crane which had given the cry was the father of the pet Crane, and learning from Mr. Fox of the starving condition d his friends, he flew to the hunting grounds of the tribe, and as there had been a good kill that day, the Crane found no trouble in securing a great quantity of fat. This he carried to the tent of Kutesan and, hovering over the tent he suddenly let the fat drop to the earth and at once the pet Crane picked it up and carried it to the woman.

Wishing to surprise the family on their awakening in the morning she got a good stick for a light, heaped up sticks on the dying embers, and started up a rousing fire and proceeded to melt the fat, as melted fat is considered a favorite dish. Although busily occupied she kept her ears open for any strange noises coming out of the forest, there being usually some enemies lurking around. She held her pan in such a position that after the fat started to melt and quite a lot of the hot grease accumulated in the pan, she could plainly see the teepee door reflected in the hot grease, as though she used a mirror.

When she had nearly completed her task, she heard a noise as though some footsteps were approaching. Instantly her heart began to beat heavily on her ribs, but she sat perfectly quiet, calling all her self control into play to keep from making an outcry. This smart woman had already studied out a way in which to best this enemy, in case an enemy it should be. The footsteps, or noise, continued to move forward, until at last the woman saw reflected in the pan of grease a hand slowly protruding through the tent door, and the finger pointed, as if counting, to the sleeping Kutesan, then to each one of the sleeping children, then to her who sat at the fire. Little did the enemy suppose that the brave woman, who sat so composed at her fire, was watching every motion he was making. The hand slowly withdrew, and as the footsteps slowly died away, there rang out on the still night air the deep fierce howl of the Prairie Wolf.

At once she aroused her husband and children. Annoyed at being so abruptly disturbed from his deep sleep, the husband crossly asked why she had awakened him so roughly. The wife explained what she had seen and heard. She at once pinned an old blanket around the Crane's shoulders and an old piece of Buffalo hide on his head for a hat or head covering. Heaping piles of wood onto the fire she instructed him to run around outside of the hut until the family returned, as they were going to see if they could find some roots to mix up with the fat. Hurriedly she tied her blanket around her middle, put her baby inside of it, and then grabbed her three year old son and packed him on her back. Kutesan also hurriedly packed the next two and the older boy took care of himself.

Immediately upon leaving the tent they took three different directions, to meet again on the high hill west of their home. The reflection from the fire in the tent disclosed to them the poor pet Crane running around the tent. It looked exactly like a child with its blanket and hat on.

Suddenly there rang out a score of shots and war whoops of the dreaded Crow Indians. Finding the tent deserted they disgustedly filed off and were swallowed up in the darkness of the deep forest.

The next morning the family returned to see what had become of their pet Crane. There, riddled to pieces, lay the poor bird who had given up his life to save his dear friends.

THE LEGEND OF THE DREAM CATCHER

(Dakota)

Long ago when the world was young an old Lakota spiritual leader was on a high mountain and had a vision. In this vision, Iktomi, the great trickster and teacher of wisdom, appeared in the form of a Spider. Iktomi, the Spider picked up the Elder's willow hoop which had feathers, horsehair, beads and offerings on it, and began to spin a web. Iktomi spoke to the Elder about the cycles of life; how we begin our lives as infants, move on through childhood and onto adulthood. Finally, we go to the old age where we must be taken care of as infants, completing the cycle.

"But," Iktomi said as he continued to spin his web, "in each time of life there are many forces; some good and some bad. If you listen to the good forces, they will steer you in the right direction. But, if you listen to the bad forces, they'll steer you in the wrong direction, and may hurt you. So these forces can help or can interfere with the harmony of Nature."

While the Spider spoke, he continued to weave his web. When Iktomi finished speaking, he gave the Elder the web and said, "The web is a perfect circle with a hole in the center. Use the web to help your people reach their goals, make good use of their ideas, dreams and visions. If you believe in the Great Spirit, the web will catch your good ideas and the bad ones will go through the hole."

The Elder passed on his vision to the people, and now many Indian's hang a dream catcher above their bed to sift their dreams and visions. The good is captured in the web of life and carried with the people, but the evil in their dreams drops through the hole in the center of the web and are no longer a part of their lives.

THE RACCOON AND THE CRAWFISH

(Sioux)

Sharp and cunning is the raccoon, say the Indians, by whom he is named Spotted Face.

A Crawfish one evening wandered along a river bank, looking for something dead to eat. A Raccoon was also out looking for something to eat spied the Crawfish and formed a plan to catch him.

He lay down on the bank and pretended to be dead. By and by the Crawfish came nearby.

"Ho," he thought, "here is a feast indeed; but is he really dead. I will go near and pinch him with my claws and find out."

So he went near and pinched the Raccoon on the nose and then on his soft paws. The Raccoon never moved. The Crawfish then pinched him on the ribs and tickled him so that the Raccoon could hardly keep from laughing. The Crawfish at last left him.

"The Raccoon is surely dead," he thought. And he hurried back to the Crawfish village and reported his find to the Chief.

All the villagers were called to go down to the feast. The Chief bade the warriors and young men to paint their faces and dress in their best for a dance.

So they marched in a long line, first the warriors, with their weapons in hand, then the women with their babies and children, to the place where the Raccoon lay.

They formed a great circle about him and danced, singing, "We shall have a great feast, on the Spotted Faced beast, with soft smooth paws. "He is dead! "He is dead! "We shall dance! "We shall have a good time; "We shall feast on his flesh."

But as they danced, the Raccoon suddenly jumped to his feet.

“Who is that you say you are going to eat? He has a Spotted Face, has he? He has soft, smooth paws, has he? I’ll break your ugly backs. I’ll break your rough bones. I’ll crunch your ugly, rough paws.” And the Raccoon rushed among the Crawfish, killing them by scores. The Crawfish warriors fought bravely and the women ran screaming, all to no purpose. They did not feast on the Raccoon but the raccoon did feasted on them!

AT THE RAINBOW'S END

(Navajo)

Long, long ago when First Woman the Goddess was created, she became fully grown in four days. It seemed that every Navajo Indian tribesman wanted her for his wife.

She did not love any of them, but she did like the handsome braves. Of all the braves, however, she thought the most attractive was the Sun God. Of course, she thought he could never be her husband.

To her surprise, one day Sun God came up behind her and gently tickled her neck with a feather. She was surrounded with warm sunshine, and in a magical way the Goddess became the wife of Sun God. He fathered her firstborn, a son.

Not long thereafter, the Goddess was resting beneath an overhanging cliff when some drops of water fell upon her. Soon the Goddess gave birth to a second son, fathered by Water God. Because the two boys were so close in age, they became known as the Twins of the Goddess.

They lived in a beautiful canyon that later became a part of Navajo land. About that time, a Great Giant roamed over the country and ate every human he could catch. He discovered the Goddess but did not want to kill her, because at first sight he fell in love with her beauty.

The Goddess knew of the Great Giant's evil ways and would have nothing to do with him. The Great Giant became very jealous of her when he saw footprints of the Twins outside her lodge.

She saw Great Giant approaching, so she quickly dug a hole in the center of her floor and there hid her two children, whom she dearly loved. She covered the opening with a flat sandstone rock, spreading dirt over it to prevent the Great Giant from finding her Twins.

Another day, Great Giant saw the children's tracks.

"Where did these children come from?" he asked the Goddess.

"I have no children." she replied, because she knew that he would try to kill them if he found the Twins.

"You are not telling me the truth," he said. "I see children's footprints in the dirt, right here."

The Goddess laughed heartily and said "Those are only my hand prints. I am very lonesome for children, so I only pretend by making tracks with the heels of my hand and the tips of my fingers, like this. These are the tracks of my children."

"Now I believe you," he replied.

As the Twins grew larger, their mother could not hide them any longer. She was worried about their safety because of the Great Giant, who saw them one day and tried to catch them. But the Twins were too quick and got away.

The Spirit who made the Goddess appeared with a bow made of cedar wood for Sun Child.

"It is time for you to learn to hunt," she said to him.

"We must now make some arrows and another bow for your brother," said the Goddess to Sun Child.

"Mostly, we want to hunt for our father," said Sun Child. "Mother, who is our father and where does he live?"

"Your father is the Sun God, but he lives far away in the East," replied the Goddess.

Another bow was made for Water Child and many arrows for both Twins. They began their journey to the East and travelled as far as they could, but without success in finding Sun God.

When they returned they asked, "Mother, have you lied to us? In the East, we looked everywhere and we could not find our father, the Sun God."

"He must have gone to the South," she said. Again the Twins set out on another journey, this time to the South, returning without success.

"Please try the West and then the North, if at first you do not find your father in the West," said the Goddess.

She sent the Twins again on their hunting journey, nervous to keep them away and out of sight of the Great Giant. Many moons later, the Twins came back and said, "Mother, have you lied to us four times? Our father was neither in the North nor the West."

"Now I will tell you the truth, my sons," said the Goddess. "Your fathers, the Sun God and Water God, live far away in the middle of the great Western Water. Between here and there are great canyons where the walls of the cliffs clap together and would crush you."

"Even if you should succeed in getting through the canyons, there are the terrible reeds that you must cross. Their long knife like sharp leaves will cut you into pieces."

"If you should escape the reeds, you can never cross the Grand Canyon, which comes first before you can reach the Great Water. You can never, never cross the water where your father's house is in the middle of the Great Water, the Western Ocean."

"But, Mother, we want to go and try to find our fathers," said the Twins.

The Goddess taught the Twins a song of protection for their next journey.

"We are travelling in an Invisible Way to seek our fathers, the Sun God and the Water God."

This song she taught them to sing four times, the magic number. Day after day as they travelled along, they sang their song for protection.

One day, as they passed a little Spider hole in the ground, they heard a voice say, “Ssh!” four times. The Twins looked into the hole and saw Spider Woman.

“Do not be afraid of me, I am your Grandmother. Come down into my lodge,” she said four times.

“We cannot enter your lodge, because your doorway is too small,” said the Twins.

“Please blow toward the Eastwind, Southwind, Westwind, and Northwind,” Spider Woman called out.

The Twins blew in the four directions and the entrance enlarged enough for them to go through. Inside and to their surprise, they saw the lodge walls covered with bundles of bones wrapped in spider webs, exactly the way Spiders wrap Flies in a web.

“Do not be afraid, my grandsons,” said Spider Woman. “These are the bones of bad men whom I killed.”

Spider Woman talked with the Twins about things that they might come across on their trip. She taught them songs for their protection and explained what they could do to overcome problems they might meet on their way.

“I will give each of you a magic Feather. Hold it before you as you travel, straight up or sideways to carry you safely forward,” she said to the Twins.

“Be on the lookout for a little man with a red head and a striped back. He will resemble a Sand Scorpion, only a little larger, about the size of a Cricket,” she explained.

“Thank you, Grandmother, we’ll be on our way,” said the Twins.

Many days later, the Twins heard a voice from the ground. It was from the little man with the red head.

“Do not disrespect me because I am so small,” he said. “I can and want to help you. Put your hands down on the ground and spit into them four times. Now close your fists, saving the spit until you come to the Big Water. There you can wash off the spit."

The Twins did exactly as they were told, and after thanking the little man with the red head, they again began their travel. Soon the canyon walls that smashed together loomed ahead of them.

They repeated Spider Woman's prayers, holding the Feather sideways. As they moved forward the clapping walls stopped long enough to allow the Twins to walk through safely.

When they came to the area of sharp reeds, again they sang the song Spider Woman taught them, touching the tops of the reeds with their Feather. Behold! The reeds turned into cattails, which pleased the reeds so much that they quickly opened a wide path for the Twins to pass through.

Another puzzling encounter for the Twins was the giant cliff. They walked around and around its rim, making a complete circle and finally returning to their starting place.

They were making no forward progress, so they sang songs taught them by their mother and Spider Woman. They prayed over and over again. When they opened their eyes, a beautiful Rainbow appeared, creating a large bridge for them to cross over the Grand Canyon of the Colorado River.

After this magnificent adventure, the Twins continued west for a long time, until they saw the Great Water before them. The Water spread so far, they wondered, "How can we ever reach the Turquoise House of Sun God, which we know is in the middle of the Great Water?"

The Twins walked down to the beach to the edge of the water and washed the spit off their hands, singing and praying at the same time.

Behold! The Rainbow appeared again! A long Rainbow Bridge stretched before them from the beach to the Turquoise House.

Onto the Rainbow Bridge the Twins raced happily, and found their two fathers, the Sun God and the Water God, who welcomed them in the Turquoise House at the end of the Rainbow Bridge.

GHOST OF WHITE DEER

(Chickasaw)

A brave, young warrior for the Chicaksaw Nation fell in love with the daughter of a Chief. The Chief did not like the young man, who was called Blue Jay. So the Chief requested a price for the bride that he was sure that Blue Jay could not pay.

"Bring me the hide of the White Deer," said the Chief. "The Chickasaws believed that animals that were all white were sacred. The price for my daughter is one White Deer." Then the Chief laughed. The Chief knew that an all White Deer, an albino, was very rare and would be very hard to find. White Deerskin was the best skin to use in a wedding dress, and the best White Deer skin came from the albino Deer.

Blue Jay went to his beloved, whose name was Bright Moon. "I will return with your bride price in one moon, and we will be married. This I promise you." Taking his best bow and his sharpest arrows Blue Jay went to hunt the White Deer.

Three weeks went by, and Blue Jay was often hungry, lonely, and scratched by many briars. Then, one night during a full moon, Blue Jay saw a White Deer that seemed to float through the moonlight. When the Deer was very close to where Blue Jay hid, he shot his sharpest arrow. The arrow sank deep into the Deer's heart. But instead of sinking to his knees to die, the deer began to run. Instead of running away, the deer began to run toward Blue Jay, his red eyes glowing, his horns sharp and frightening.

A month passed and Blue Jay did not return as he had promised Bright Moon. As the months dragged by, the tribe decided that he would never return.

But Bright Moon never took any other young man as a husband, for she had a secret. When the Moon was shinning as brightly as her name, Bright Moon would often see the White Deer in the smoke of the campfire, running, with an arrow in his heart. She lived hoping the Deer would finally fall, and Blue Jay would return.

To this day the White Deer is sacred to the Chickasaw People, and the White Deerskin is still the favorite skin for the wedding dress.

THE LEGEND OF DEVIL'S TOWER

(Sioux)

Out of the plains of Wyoming rises Devil's Tower. It is really a rock, visible for a hundred miles around, an huge cone of basalt which seems to touch the clouds. It sticks out of the flat prairie as if someone had pushed it up from underground.

Of course, Devil's Tower is a white man's name. Indians have no devil in their beliefs and got along well all these many centuries without him. White Man invented the devil and, as far as the Indians are concerned, the White Man can keep him. But everybody these days knows that towering rock by this name, so Devil's Tower it is. Most tribes call it Bear Rock because of its sheer sides many, many streaks and gashes running straight up and down, like scratches made by giant claws.

Well, long, long ago, two young Indian boys found themselves lost in the prairie. They had played shinny ball and whacked it a few hundred yards out of the village. And then they had shot their bows still farther out into the sagebrush. And then they had heard a small animal make a noise and had gone to investigate. They had come to a stream with many colorful pebbles and followed that for a while. They had come to a hill and wanted to see what was on the other side. On the other side they saw a herd of Antelope and, of course, had to track them for a while. When they got hungry and thought it was time to go home, the two boys found that they didn't know where they were. They started off in the direction they thought their village was, but only got farther away from it. At last they curled up beneath a tree and went to sleep.

They got up the next morning and walked some more, still headed the wrong way. They ate some wild berries and dug up wild turnips, found some choke cherries, and drank water from streams. For three days they walked toward the West. Their feet were sore, but they survived. Oh, how they wished that their parents, or aunts and uncles, or elder brothers and sisters would find them. But nobody did.

On the fourth day the boys suddenly had a feeling that they were being followed. They looked around and in the distance saw Mato, the Bear. This was no ordinary Bear, but a giant Grizzly Bear so huge that the boys would make only a small mouthful for him, but he had smelled the boys and wanted that mouthful. He kept coming close, and the earth trembled as he gathered speed.

The boys started running, looking for a place to hide, but here was no such place and the Grizzly Bear was much, much faster than they. They stumbled, and the Grizzly Bear was almost upon them. They could see his red, wide open jaws full of giant, evil teeth. They could smell his hot evil breath.

The boys were old enough to have learned to pray, and the called upon Wakan Tanka, the Creator, "Tunkashila, Grandfather, have pity, save us."

All at once the earth shook and began to rise. The boys rose with it. Out of the earth came a cone of rock going up, up up until it more than a thousand feet high and the boys were on top of it.

Mato the Bear was disappointed to see his meal disappearing into the clouds. This Grizzly Bear was so huge that he could almost reach to the top of the rock when he stood on his hind legs, but not quite. His claws were as large as a teepee's lodge poles. Frantically Mato the Bear dug his claws into the side of the rock, trying to get up, trying to get those boys. As he did so, he made big scratches in the sides of the towering rock. He tried every spot, every side. He scratched up the rock all around, but it was no use. They boys watched him tiring himself out, getting mad, and giving up. They finally saw him going away, a huge, growling, grunting mountain of Grizzly Bear disappearing over the horizon.

The boys were saved. Or were they? How were they to get down? They were humans, not birds who could fly. They were stranded on that giant basalt cone.

So how did the two boys get down? The legend does not say, but be sure that the Great Spirit didn't save those boys only to let them die of hunger and thirst on the top of the rock.

Well, the Eagle has always been a friend to our people. So it must have been the Eagle that let the boys grab hold of him and carried them safely back to their village.

ORIGIN OF ANIMALS

(Apache)

When the Apaches emerged from the underworld, they traveled southward on foot for four days. They had no other food than the seeds of the two plants, from which they made a sort of flour by grinding between stones. When they camped for the fourth day, one of the teepees, stood somewhat apart from the others. While the warrior and his wife were absent from his lodge, a Raven brought a bow and a quiver of arrows, and hung them upon the lodge poles. The children within took down the quiver, and found some meat in it; they ate this, and at once became very fat. When the mother returned, she saw the grease on the hands and cheeks of the children, and was told how the fat had been obtained. The woman hastened to her husband with the tale.

Surprised by the appearance of the children, the people gathered to await the reappearance of the Raven which brought such remarkable food. When the Raven found the fat had been stolen from the quiver, he flew away toward the Eastward; his destination was a mountain just beyond the range of vision of the Indians. A Bat, however, followed the flight of the Raven, and informed them where the Raven had alighted. That night, a council of the tribe was held, and it was decided that they should go to the home of the Raven, and try to obtain from him the food which had wrought such an unbelievable change in those children who ate it. At the end of fourth day they came to a place where a large number of logs were lying in irregular mass. Many Ravens were seen, but they avoided the Indians, and no information could be obtained from them. At one point they discovered a great circle of ashes where the Ravens had cooked their meals. Again a council was held, and they talked over the problem of how to spy upon the Ravens, and learn where they obtained the valuable animal food. That night the Medicine Men transformed a boy into a Puppy, and concealed him in the bushes near the camp. After the Indians had departed, next morning, the Ravens came, as is their habit, to examine the abandoned camp.

One of the young Ravens found the Puppy, and was so pleased with it that he exclaimed "This shall be my Puppy."

When he carried home his Puppy his parents told him to throw it away. He begged permission to keep it, but agreed to give it up if the Puppy winked when a chip of burning wood was waved before its eyes. Since the Puppy possessed much more than canine intelligence, it stared during the test without the quiver of an eyelid. So the young Raven got to keep the Puppy, which he placed under his own blanket, where it remained until evening. At sunset the Puppy peeped from his cover, and saw an old Raven brush aside the ashes of the fireplace, and take up a large flat stone which disclosed an opening beneath; through this he disappeared, but arose again with a Buffalo, which was killed and eaten by the Ravens.

For four days the Puppy remained at the camp of the Ravens, and each evening he saw a Buffalo brought up from the depths and eaten. Satisfied that he had discovered the source from which the Ravens got their food, the puppy changed back into a boy on the morning of the fifth day, and, with a White Eagle feather in one hand and a Black Eagle feather one in the other, crawled through the opening beneath the fireplace, as he had seen the Ravens do. In the underworld in which he found himself he saw four Buffaloes. He placed the White Eagle feather in the mouth of the nearest Buffalo, and commanded it to follow him, but the Buffalo told him to go on to the last of the four and take it. This the boy tried to do, but the fourth Buffalo sent him back to the first, in whose mouth the boy again thrust the feather, declaring it to be the king of animals.

He then returned to the world above, followed by the four Buffalo. As the Buffalo passed through the hole, one of the Ravens, and hastened to clap down the stone covering the opening, but he was too late to prevent their escape.

Seeing that they had passed from his control into that of Red Man, he exclaimed, "When you kill any of these Buffalo you must at least leave their eyes for me."

Attended by the four Buffalo, the boy followed the tracks made by the departing Apaches. On the site of their first camp he found a firestick of which he asked, "When did my people leave here?"

"Three days ago," was the firestick. At the next camping place was an abandoned ladder, of which he asked, "When did my people leave here?"

"Two days ago," replied the ladder. Continuing his journey the boy soon reached the third camping place, where he questioned another firestick, and learned that the people had been gone but one day. At the fourth camp another ladder answered his question, with the news that the Indians had left there that morning. That evening he overtook them and entered the camp with the four Buffalo following him.

One old woman who lived in a brush lodge became angry at one of the Buffalo who knocked over her rude shelter. Snatching up a stick from the fire, she struck the Buffalo over the nose.

"Hereafter you shall avoid mankind; your nose will tell you when you are near them," said she. This ended the brief period of harmony between man and the Buffalo. The Buffalo left the camp at once, going farther each day, until on the fourth they disappeared from sight. That night the Apaches prayed for the return of the Buffalo, that they might use them for food, and that is why Buffalo only come near camps now at night. They never come very close, because the old woman told them to be guided by their noses and avoid the Indians.

www.ingramcontent.com/pod-product-compliance
Lightning Source LLC
LaVergne TN
LVHW060823170826
845678LV00010B/1880
9798668237685